Lord, Did You Cry With Me When Mommy Hit Me?

Nancy Stokkermans

Copyright 2013 by MSI Press, LLC

All rights reserved. No part of this book may be reproduced or utilized in any form or by any means, electronic or mechanical, including photocopying, recording, or by any information storage and retrieval system, without permission in writing from the publisher.

For information, contact:

MSI Press
1760-F Airline Highway, 203
Hollister, CA 95023
Orders@MSIPress.com
Telephone/Fax: 831-886-2486

Library of Congress Control Number 2013945230

ISBN: 978-1-933455-34-1

Cover design by Carl Leaver

*I dedicate this book to my loving sister Kathy,
whose kindness and love touches everyone's heart.
May God bless and protect her forever!*

Contents

Introduction 7
Cast of Characters..13
Dark Days..21
Light in the Dark 29
Angels on Earth 37
When Pain Begets Joy 45
The Catalyst..55
Young Love 65
Growing Up All of a Sudden 75
Charting my own map..87
Seeing the Whole Picture 95
What Worked for Me 103
Afterword... 117

Introduction

We think sometimes that poverty is only being hungry, naked and homeless. The poverty of being unwanted, unloved and uncared for is the greatest poverty. We must start in our own homes to remedy this kind of poverty.
—Mother Teresa

Imagine a cold March night with stubborn snow still stuck to the sides of the road and heavy flakes hitting the windshield of an unheated car as it drives toward the city. In the back seat, a fifteen-year-old girl moans quietly in pain. It is a pain unlike any she has ever known, but she is afraid to cry out. In the front seat, a man and a woman—her parents—sit in stony silence. They hear her stifled moans and refuse to offer comfort.

Something trickles between her legs. She dabs it with her fingers. Is it blood? She is afraid. She is having a baby.

They hear her sobs and feel she deserves this pain. She will have this baby alone. She will be punished.

Her father floors the gas pedal. Let's get this over with, he thinks. The car's headlights illuminate the snowflakes, and for a moment it looks as though the car is floating in space.

At the hospital entrance, he opens the door and pulls her out. She stumbles toward a nurse, who reaches out to her. When she turns around, her father is gone. The car is gone. She is alone.

***

The girl in the back seat is my sister, Kathy. The people who left her at the hospital are my parents.

My name is Nancy Stokkermans, and this is my story.

***

I grew up in a house in the country. From the outside, it looked unremarkable, but to me and my siblings, it was a war zone. My father was an alcoholic who loved no one, not even himself, and my mother was so deeply unhappy that she would explode in violent rage at the slightest provocation—or even with no provocation at all.

Like I said: a warzone. I would walk across my own living room floor and step on a landmine. One minute, I'd be a six-year-old girl carrying a doll to the sofa and the next I'd be thrown up against a wall, my nose bloodied. I'd never know what had happened or why. It was just the way things were in my house.

My parents had six children: Ken is the oldest, then Kathy, Karen, me, Gordon, and finally Donna. For some people, to bear even one baby is an impossible dream, but my parents were blessed with six healthy, beautiful children. The irony is that they were both unequipped to be parents at all.

A typical Sunday in our house went like this: the sun would dawn on a relatively peaceful household, and my mother would attempt to make breakfast for the family. Within minutes of my father's arrival in the kitchen, however, the tension would begin to mount. My father would open up one of the brown bottles he was always drinking from—I wouldn't realize what was in them until I was nearly in my teens—and his mood would descend with each sip. He would begin to argue with my mother, who would begin to cry. He would lose patience with her show of emotion; she would get angry at his intolerance. This would escalate until my father stormed off alone with his brown bottle, not to be seen for the rest of the day, and my mother would abandon the breakfast and go looking for my sister Kathy.

I don't know why she chose Kathy as her target, but my older sister, Mom's second child, was the focus of almost all her resentment and rage. Whenever Mom felt upset, which happened several times every day, she would hunt Kathy down and beat her brutally. She would strike from behind; Kathy, sitting at the dining-room table doing homework, innocent and unsuspecting, would feel a hard strike on the back of her head. She'd turn around to find out what was happening only to have her face slapped so hard she'd fall off her chair. "You stupid kid!" my mom would scream at her. "Get off your ass and clean the kitchen—now!"

***

I talk about these things now, and I know what they mean. My siblings and I were the victims of serious trauma and abuse. I have met with therapists, and I have searched my soul as an adult, so I understand the implications of all that I went through. *Now* I do. But then? I was a child, and I had no point of reference, none at all. So, I thought all of this was normal. Imagine it: I had no idea that there was anything wrong with the picture. I thought everyone had a father who could go for weeks without saying a word to his daughter. I thought every mother beat her children mercilessly. I thought nothing of the fact that my older sister had bruises on her body nearly every day of her young life. I thought it was a normal act of discipline to be thrown into the tiny crawl space under the house. While other kids were taking time outs in a corner of the living room, we were being shoved into this dank, windowless dungeon where we could feel, but not see, the rats that skittered over our ankles. I didn't think this was strange.

***

Our memories have a way of distorting the past, filtering out details so that only foggy portraits remain. Some events, though, get preserved with crystal-clear accuracy. I remember one particular incident that happened when I was about ten years old. I had been jumping on the bed, and it had broken. My father was in the process of fixing it, and I decided to help him since I was the one who had broken it. As I walked around the mess, I accidentally stepped on a nail that protruded out of the bed frame. It imbedded itself deep in my heel. The pain was excruciating, of course; I was a brave kid, but I nearly fainted, especially when I had to pull my foot off of the nail slowly, my blood pooling on the floor. I looked up at my dad, stricken, hoping beyond hope for some comfort from this man, but it was not to be had. "How stupid can you be?" he screamed. Coming from a man who rarely spoke to me, these words were crushing. I ran from the room and bolted outside and down the long laneway. I didn't stop until I reached the creek far from my house. I ran without shoes on, bleeding from my foot. I sat with my foot in the rushing water, hoping the bleeding would stop. I sat there and cried myself empty.

***

Every day in my house was hard, but Sundays, for some reason, were the worst. Was it because my father was an atheist, and my mother was a thwarted Christian? Was it that the absence of any spiritual foundation in our home brought people's emotional tensions to a boil on that particular day? I don't know, but I remember Sundays as the most painful day of the week. It was the day my father started drinking before the breakfast dishes were cleared away; it was the day my mother cried herself into a stupor. Most people say they don't like Mondays, but I was always relieved to see the sunrise on Monday morning: it meant we had survived Sunday even if we were battered and bruised.

***

My childhood was hard, yes. The suffering continued, as you will see in the coming chapters, but all along, I had an inkling that God was with me even when it seemed most unlikely. I knew that even though my own parents couldn't love me, there was someone, somewhere, who did. I sensed God even before I knew who He was. In the darkest moments, when all I could hear was the sound of my own breathing in the damp cold of the crawl space or the sobs of my sister as she nursed her freshest wounds, I knew there was someone to live for, and I dedicated myself to finding Him, however long it might take.

Nancy Stokkermans

1
Cast of Characters

My family was large—two adults and six children, plus one grandchild. So, I will paint a quick portrait of each person.

Ken was the first child born to my parents. I don't know whether they planned his birth or not, but I must suppose that they were happy to have him. At least, my mother was. She doted on him from the moment he was born and continues to do so to this day. What's so strange about that, you might ask. What mother doesn't want to dote on her eldest son? Well, let me explain: Ken is not exactly a "golden boy." He is not the loveable little imp with a mischievous glint in his eye. No, Ken has been, for as long as I can possibly remember, a selfish, violent thug with no regard for anyone but himself. He frequently and casually hurt all of us, including my mother, yet she never had anything but affection for him. She forgave his most terrible sins, some of which were very dark indeed—I will describe them in upcoming chapters—and she defended him when anyone dared speak against him. My father often dared: by the time Ken was an older child, he and my father were nearly enemies. While Ken could never supplant my father as the patriarch of the household, he certainly had a lot of weight in the family. In fact, he was like a rabid dog who had taken up residence in the living room: we all knew he would snarl as we walked past and could attack at any moment, but we all had to live with him, anyway. My mother would coddle him, stroking his matted hair, even as he frothed at the mouth, even as he bit her hand. I feared Ken as a child, but I hated him more than I feared him. Now, as an adult, I have nothing to do with him.

The second child born to my family was Kathy. As vicious as Ken has always been, Kathy has been gentle. As selfish as he was, she was considerate. Perhaps this is the lot of the second child. Quite often, they are calmer and more diplomatic than their firstborn siblings. In that, Kathy was exceptional. She was a shrinking violet not only by virtue of her second-born status but also because she was diminished every day by the abuse from my mother, the neglect from my father and the bulling from Ken. Kathy was their victim from the day she was born. Poor, sweet Kathy! She never stood a chance. She was their punching bag, and no one took more advantage of this than my mother. She beat Kathy daily. You could set your watch by it. Looking back, that might have been the most reliable element in my life. I couldn't always count on getting breakfast or having a safe place to sleep, but I could count on hearing the *thwack* of my mother's hand against Kathy's face, on seeing Kathy furtively wipe the blood from her mouth. Why did my mother target Kathy in particular? I don't know; I'll probably never know. I ask the question often, but Kathy is defined by it. Miraculously, though, Kathy has become one of the strongest people I know. She was destroyed by her parents—all but murdered, and surely they murdered a big part of her spirit—but somehow she stands tall today. She is loving and giving; she is good to her own children. She nurtures them; her hands are gentle on their cheeks. Yes, Kathy will still flinch if you raise your voice, and she has the comportment of a shy, trembling schoolgirl, but her soul is strong, and she is radiant with goodwill. Somehow, by a miracle greater than any I can fathom, Kathy took the hate that was fed to her every day and turned it into love.

Lord, Did You Cry With Me When Mommy Hit Me?

Karen came next. She was a happy child, in spite of our difficult life. It sounds strange, but I relate to Karen's demeanor because I was the same: I was a happy child. We both endured a lot of abuse from our parents, and we both watched Kathy suffer. We were, nonetheless, blessed with the ability to find joy wherever it was hiding, even if it was hiding in the crawl space with the rats. Of course, after a lifetime of living in our house, Karen's sunny disposition was clouded with anger, and that anger grew deeper over the years. One thing she always wanted but never got was to be "daddy's girl," the perfect daughter in our father's eyes. She strove for his attention. She worked hard at it, but the only attention he ever gave her was when he needed something done: a bill paid, a phone call made, a chore completed. I think it's safe to say that Karen received more of our father's love than any of the rest of us, but that's still not saying much. He wasn't able to give out more than a drip at a time, and she was thirstier than anyone. Karen was the first child born after Kathy and she often found herself wedged between the rock and the hard place that were Kathy and Mom. She stopped some pretty awful things from happening to Kathy, and I can only imagine the pressure she must have felt. My parents gave Karen too many adult responsibilities from a very early age, and of her own accord she assumed the responsibility of protecting Kathy. I think the burden of these duties took their toll on Karen over the years.

After Karen came Gordon. He was a sweet baby and a caring child. Like Karen and me, he managed to find kernels of happiness amid the chaos and to hoard them and protect them. Unlike Karen and me, however, Gord seems to have forgotten the bad about our childhood and remembers only the good. When I talk about it with him now, he says he can't remember ever being beaten by Mom, and his memories of Dad are all positive. He does remember being on the receiving end of the strap from time to time, but he feels we must have deserved whatever punishments we got. This is fascinating to me, that

Gord can remember things so differently, that he has reconciled his past so completely. I have to wonder: is this a willful amnesia? Has Gord suppressed these memories because they are too traumatizing? Or did he really experience childhood as an unremarkable, relatively peaceful time? One thing Gord does remember, mind you, is Ken. He remembers Ken as vile. There's no amnesia there: the violent, scary, cruel, and perverted things Ken did are forever etched in Gord's memory, and to this day he avoids Ken even though they live in the same small town.

Next in the birth order, the second-to-last child, was me. I was named Nancy after the nurse who delivered me. I'm thankful to this day that the nurse wasn't named something like Taffy or Brunhilde!

The last baby born to my parents was Donna, a dark-haired, pink-cheeked little beauty. I was thrilled to have her. A baby to love and play with, someone smaller than me! Growing up, Donna and I spent a lot of time playing together. We didn't always get along, but we had fun. I remember long summer days building houses with her out of the long grasses that grew nearby. Donna was the youngest member of a large family, and that must have been a tough job. One of the only ways she knew to get attention from our parents was to tattle on us. This was a bad bargain because she'd win their favor only to lose ours! Donna suffered many health issues as a child, which meant my mother was inclined to dote on her—but only when she was sick. The rest of the time, our mother was her usual cruel self. It must have been so confusing for Donna, who was so little, to navigate between these moods.

***

There are two more people on this stage, and although they may not deserve much applause, they should have their moment in the spotlight. My parents both have life stories that tug at the heartstrings. Each of them could have written a book!

They came by their failures honestly. Indeed, all people are the quotient of the events of their past, and my parents' pasts—their lives before they were parents—were certainly riddled with hardships. That they never transcended these hardships is their fault, but the suffering each of them endured in the first place happened when they were as innocent as the rest of us.

My father was a reticent man, so what I knew about him I learned slowly, by hints and innuendo, over the years. His life was a hard one before he ever met my mother, and I suppose he expected it to improve once he got married and started a family. He was entirely too familiar with loss and grief from a very early age. First, he lost his twin brother at birth. Then, his only sister developed a brain tumor along with a brain aneurism at the age of six. She managed to live through that but died at a young age not long after she had her children. Dad contracted polio when he was in his twenties and had to spend countless hours wearing a brace and doing excruciating physiotherapy. His only brother went off to war when my dad was young. He also lost a lot of friends in the war, yet was unable to go off to war himself— something he dearly wanted to do—because of his polio. Finally, both of dad's parents died before he was eighteen. His mother died of a disease that they call today Lou Gehrig's disease, and his father died of an asthma attack while my father was holding him in his arms. These tragedies separated him from his siblings. My father stayed with his uncle, and his brother and sister were taken in by an aunt. So, he was no stranger to tragedy and had already experienced more of it by the time of his high school prom than most of us will experience in a lifetime. It is no great surprise that he turned to alcohol or even that he turned away from his family. A stronger man would have risen from the ashes of this life and turned things around, but weakened by his miseries, my father crumbled. He turned more deeply inward with every passing year, and the sadness inside him took up residence next to his despair. There was no room for anything else.

My mother's past is equally painful and equally obscure to me. Although she was always more open than my father and talked to me about her past, I know there are things she won't tell me: skeletons in her closet too gruesome to reveal. I can only guess what they might look like, but the things I know for certain are bad enough. For one thing, my mother lived with her immediate family, grandparents, aunts and uncles and their children along with a hired hand. A difficult arrangement at best, love for one child-mom-was hard to find when there was so much work to be accomplished each and every day. When the families decided to separate and find homes of their own, Mom was left behind with her grandmother. She had made that choice for two important reasons, the first being she had no choice; the decision was made by her parents. The second reason was that her one sister detested her, treating Mom maliciously and despicably. One example of such behavior happened when her sister forced Mom's finger into a meat grinder and laughed as she did so, leaving Mom's finger disfigured to this day. Mom's sister Barb and her brother Gordy also stayed behind because of proximity to their school but soon after left to stay with their biological parents, leaving Mom behind. My mother loved her grandmother dearly and relished the time she spent with her, but it must have felt just awful to be considered "surplus" by your own parents. She was the only daughter who was sent away, and she had to live with the knowledge that her very existence was too much for her parents to bear. My mother's father was an alcoholic, and from what I can tell, he was a frightening, angry one. It is certainly no coincidence that Mom married an alcoholic later on, but it is an eerie coincidence indeed that these two men in her life had the same name: both her father and her husband were named William John. Too bad she couldn't take the hint: She married a man who was unable to love her, who reinforced the dysfunctional cycle of her life, who kept her locked in the house of rage and resentment she had built for herself.

Lord, Did You Cry With Me When Mommy Hit Me?

***

And then there's me, Nancy. Born fifth, I joined the family when the party was in full swing. I always had a knack for observation, and sometimes I would stop and watch my family like they were actors in a play on stage. I could see the interactions between characters; I could see the way the plot was unfolding. Sometimes I would cringe at the dialogue; sometimes I would wish for an intermission. I feel that over the years, I honed my skills as an observer of human dynamics, of family interplay, and that's one of the things that helped me write this book. Another, of course, is God.

God is the unseen character in this cast. No one could see Him there on stage, but He was there, and I knew it. I spoke to Him every night. He lived in my room with me. He lived outside in the long grass. He even lived in the dark of the basement crawlspace where I was sent when I misbehaved. He came to me and spoke softly, in eloquent soliloquies, at night before I slept. While my house was shrouded in dark, while it was briefly calmed of its turmoil, God came to me, and decades later, when I was fully grown, God came to me again in the quiet of my bedroom at night. He spoke again. This time, I could hear His words clearly because I knew how to listen: *Nancy*, He said, *it's time for you to share everything I've shown you with the world. It's time for you to share your journey. I want you to write a book.*

Nancy Stokkermans

2
Dark Days

Even though God was a part of my life from as early as I can remember, I can't exactly say I recognized or appreciated His companionship. I was a child: I had simple, concrete needs, and most of the time they weren't being met. The concept of God was too abstract to be comforting in my day-to-day misery. I was still so young that I could only imagine comfort coming from my parents, and it definitely wasn't coming from there.

My mother read the *Bible* to us almost every day. She would sit us down at the kitchen table and read a paragraph or two from the New Testament. My father, of course, was never in on these sessions. If she picked up the Bible while he was around, he scoffed and left the room, but my mom went on undeterred. Since this was the only book she read to any of us, we ate it up—children love to be read to. She probably could have read us the obituary section of the newspaper, and we'd have been thrilled just to have her reading to us! The stories in the *Bible*, though, made me feel at once peaceful and hopeful. How I wished to meet someone like this man named Jesus! Surely, He would take me on his lap and cuddle me. Surely, His beard would scratch my forehead. He would play games with me and my siblings; He could push me in the tire swing out front. This

Jesus character was just wonderful, and my mother told us we could pray to Him.

In my room, at night I prayed: "Oh, Jesus, please come and fix my parents. Make my mom happy, make my dad love me." I would listen hard for a response, straining my ears. I would open the window so I could hear well. However, nothing was forthcoming, and I went to bed disappointed every night.

I prayed to God. I prayed to Jesus. I got silence. The feeling I had in those days was something akin to jealousy. *How can God exist but refuse to listen to me? Why won't He answer my prayers? Whose prayers is He answering instead?* How young I was! I thought I could pray in this straightforward way, like I was talking to Santa Claus.

I wouldn't learn otherwise until I was much older. In the meantime, I tried to survive. The day-to-day in my house was like an ache. It hurt constantly, but it was bearable. It was only at certain times—once a day or so—that the ache flared into a searing pain. So, for the most part I was able to limp along, aware of the ache but able to ignore it.

I spent most of each day watching my mother carefully to see if she was going to explode into a rage. Since her anger was hair-triggered and unpredictable, there was no way to gauge whether something was going to set her off. The only way to stay safe was to hover nearby and watch her face and body for signs of stress and to run away when I saw the telltale tics and signals. I would be playing in the living room with my little sister, looking at the puzzle or tower or doll that we were occupied with but always keeping one eye on my mother's profile as she sat at a kitchen chair with a magazine. I could see the muscles in her jaw from behind. If they started to tense up, I knew something was brewing. If I saw her knuckles whiten or her hands clench and unclench, I knew something was brewing. Sometimes, her shoulders would rise with each breath she took, and I'd know she was tightening up her chest. Sometimes, I could tell by the way she crossed or uncrossed her legs

Lord, Did You Cry With Me When Mommy Hit Me?

that her whole spine was getting tighter. When my mother's body changed in these subtle ways—ways most children would never notice, would never *need* to notice—I knew it was time to flee.

Usually, I made it out in time. I'd sense her building stress, and I'd leave the house before she erupted. Kathy, who was too gentle a soul, too credulous a person, to anticipate these outbursts, was usually the one in the path of the volcano. I'd hear it unfold from outside. I'd hear Mom's chair scrape on the linoleum, and I'd know she was getting up to find Kathy. Moments later, I'd hear Kathy scream.

Sometimes, though, if I was distracted or just off my game, I'd be the one who'd get caught in her path. There were certain occasions where you could say I "deserved" it, Mom's anger being the result of something I'd actually done, like the time I duct-taped my sister Donna to a tree, but most of the time her eruptions were just as random as a volcano's. When this happened, the slow ache of my life turned into a searing burn.

One of Mom's favorite punishments, and probably the most traumatizing for me, was to lock us in the crawl space below the house. This was a sort of pseudo-basement with a cold dirt floor and only enough space for a child to crouch low. It was completely dark once Mom closed the trap door on us, and there were smells I never managed to identify but will never forget. Rats lived there: it was their domain. Luckily, I always loved animals, and so I didn't have the phobia of rats that some people have—if I did I'm sure the crawl space would have been my undoing—but even an animal-lover gets squeamish when rodents she can't see are scurrying over her ankles in the dark. I never got bitten, but I couldn't help thinking of their wet, yellow teeth; and I never got sick from the rats, but I couldn't help imagining that the ground I was sitting on was made up of piles and piles of their excrement. During one of these cruel episodes, an amazing occurrence took place. I still remember it clearly to this day. I was terrified and was crying out to God to help me; my sobs went on for what seemed liked hours. Keeping my arms tucked tightly around my legs in hopes that the critters in the hole would leave me alone. Suddenly, a light appeared to my right. Words were not spoken, but somehow I could hear what the light was saying to me. More important, I felt warmth and love from the light that just hovered in the small crawl space but was much larger than the space should have allowed. At the same time, another entity entered from my left. This light was dark smoke, and it scared me even to look in its direction. Without the white light, I would not have been able to see the dark figure, but I know I will never forget the feelings that emanated from it: pure hatred and enticement to come to him. I don't know what happened during the time the two entities remained, but I do know that the dark disappeared and the light enveloped me with more love than I had ever felt before. At that time, I did not have any awareness as to what the light was. All I knew was that I was glad it was over.

I don't know how many times Mom locked me in the crawl space. Over the years, it added up to double-digits, but whether it was 15 or 50 times, I'm not sure. Indeed, it doesn't matter. Once was enough. The crawl space was so dark and damp, so utterly alienating, that it worked like a sensory-deprivation chamber and made anyone in it wonder if they were even alive. All my siblings reported the same feeling (all except Ken, who was never sent there): all of us wondered if perhaps we had died, if perhaps we had gone to hell. After an hour in the crawl space, I forgot I had fingers on the ends of my hands. I forgot that I was tall enough to climb a tree. I forgot what colors looked like or what it felt like to drink when I was thirsty. The only thing I was able to remember is what it sounded like when I cried.

Where was God while I languished in that cellar? What was He doing instead of rescuing me? What on earth could be more important? These were the questions I asked, naïve as to the complexity of the answers.

Lord, Did You Cry With Me When Mommy Hit Me?

***

The crawl space was a particularly horrific punishment, but almost all my days felt punishing in one way or another. I could make a list a mile long of the small, medium, and enormous torments my siblings and I suffered in that house, but I will let a handful of examples suffice. There was the time, which I mentioned in my introduction, when I stepped on a nail and got punished and shunned for it. There was the time my mom refused to let any of us come inside until the middle of the night—in February. There was the time my sister Kathy had the audacity to mouth off to Ken and got beaten to within an inch of her life—by Mom. And there was the time—a time that is etched into my memory in bizarre, hallucinatory bits and pieces—that I got very sick as a child.

I don't remember how it started, but I do recall that Kathy was the one who noticed my declining state and brought me to Mom. At first, Mom just scoffed. She didn't have time to look me over, and she didn't want to acknowledge Kathy's plea. Soon, though, I was pale enough and clammy enough that it got her attention. By the time she put a thermometer in my mouth, I had a fever of 105 and could no longer stand or even sit up.

Even though I was clearly very sick, I languished at home for several days, growing worse. Mom and Dad continued their drama downstairs. I could hear them fighting. They were too absorbed in their own problems to notice my faint cries from the sickbed. It wasn't until my breathing got bad—my sisters say I nearly stopped breathing altogether—that my parents finally took me to the hospital.

I was admitted immediately and diagnosed with scarlet fever, complicated by double pneumonia. The doctors told my parents to prepare for the worst. I was hooked up to numerous machines—my memory of the exact machines and procedures is foggy, but to my childish mind it felt like they were turning me into a robot—and the doctors used medicine to put me to sleep.

When I finally woke up, I was alone. I have a patchy memory of being pushed on my bed by some nurses, all of whom cooed and patted me as I whimpered myself awake. I asked for my mom. I yearned for her with a hunger like no other. I cried for her, and the nurses promised I would see her soon. However, when they brought me out of the intensive care ward, there was no one to greet me. I spent a night alone; awake, in a public room, with only strange nurses to comfort me.

When I awoke the next morning, my mother was beside me, but she was not holding my hand. She was not stroking my brow. Instead, she scowled at me. "I hope you know your father almost let you die, Nancy."

What did she mean? Why would my father do that?

"He didn't want to bother bringing you to the hospital, but if we hadn't brought you here, you would have died. Think of that, Nancy. Your father doesn't even care if you live or die."

What a thing to say. I was four years old, terrified, and ill. I had an IV in my arm and an oxygen tube up my nose. I was groggy with drugs and in desperate need of some reassurance. Instead, all I got was this random excerpt from the never-ending fight between my mom and my dad. Those words hit me deep in my heart. They still hurt today, but I knew that my mom was just angry as she spewed forth those words for the tears in her eyes rolled gently down her face. I now know she was very afraid for me.

Eventually, my mom came around and seemed happy to see me. She kissed me and hugged me, getting tangled in the IV lines. She stayed for a few hours. Dad came to pick her up and drive her home, but he didn't get out of the car. He didn't come to see me.

Mom and Dad went home that night, but I stayed at the hospital for twelve weeks. This is a lifetime to a four-year-old. It is long enough to feel like you'll never go home again, to forget what home is. Mom visited me a handful of times, but Dad never did. Mostly, I was alone, abandoned to an isolation ward with a masked nurse checking on me every once in a while. My hospital crib was like an animal's cage.

I was afraid, and I didn't understand what was happening. To my naïve mind, this was a punishment. It was no different than being locked in the crawl space. I lay awake, wondering what I had done to warrant this kind of punishment. Was it the time I snuck outside at night to look for bats? Was it the time I let baby Donna eat a whole dish of brown sugar? Was it because I kept losing mittens all winter long? Maybe it was a culmination of everything. Maybe Mom had just given up on me and sent me here.

I also wondered why I was being punished by God. What could a small child do to enrage Him so? Why would He let this happen to me, or did He *want* this to happen to me? I felt so alone. I felt abandoned by my parents and by God.

***

I was a child, and so I can be forgiven for being so short-sighted. I prayed to God, and He ignored me: it seemed like a simple equation. Maybe God really was just a story in a book. Maybe He was no different from Jack with his beanstalk or Charlie with his chocolate factory. The stubborn, insolent parts of me were tempted to believe this, but there was also a part of me that knew God was real. I couldn't say why I knew or even what, exactly, I knew, but I had a feeling. Call it faith. I decided, one day, to start paying attention to the idea that even in the darkest days, God is present. I kept this idea in my head and worked it around like a pearl.

Nancy Stokkermans

3

Light in the Dark

Important changes happen slowly. Like a glacier creeping across a frozen continent, my understanding of God was making its way into my consciousness. I grew up and away from the child I was, the child who thought God should be sitting there, waiting to hear my prayers the way someone might wait for the phone to ring. I was a child who thought I was entitled to direct, literal answers from God—and that I should get them right away. As I grew into a pre-teen, my views on this grew more complex, and I started to realize that God could listen to me without necessarily answering me and that He could answer me without necessarily giving me what I wanted.

It would take many years before these concepts became clear in my mind, but the ideas were dawning. Like I said, it began slowly and started with a deepening understanding of my own family's dynamic. I began to watch all of them with a keener eye. For example, I observed the strange relationship between Kathy and my mother. I tried to make sense of it but wondered if it was just something that simply didn't make sense; some things don't. Kathy was only a few years older than I, but from the earliest age, she was made to take care of her younger siblings. When she was three years old—still a baby, by many people's standards—she was made to dress herself and feed herself. As soon as Karen was born, Kathy was expected to help with her, too. Likewise with Gordon and me. While Mom took care of feeding us and doing most of the diaper changes, Kathy had to pick up after us and take up the slack on all the other work that Mom couldn't get to. If Mom noticed a mess, she exploded, so little Kathy patrolled the house like a soldier, cleaning up messes before they started. At an age when most kids would be making messes, oblivious to everything except the joy of their play, Kathy was cleaning them up. If she didn't, she got beaten.

By the time Donna was born, Kathy was 5 years old. Mom put too much of the responsibility for taking care of Donna on Kathy. Donna was a baby who seemed to cry all the time, and Kathy had to get up in the middle of the night to rock her. Kathy had to help change all of her diapers and help wash them. In those days we used cloth diapers out of necessity, and we had to hang them on a line since we didn't have a dryer. As anyone who has ever done it knows, taking care of a baby is a full-time job with no coffee breaks, and my sister Kathy, a child herself, was forced to take this on. How did she get paid? Well, if she did her job immaculately, she didn't get beaten. If she messed up even a little, there were bruises to show for it.

Kathy never questioned her role. From as early as she could walk or use her hands, she was made to do adult chores, and from as early as she could talk she was made to shut up and obey. There never was an option for Kathy; she knew no alternative to this life. I did, though, and I watched her suffer. What made it even more painful for me was that she seemed oblivious to her suffering. I was young, but I was not too young to see the tragedy in this: a child robbed so utterly of childhood that she never even missed it.

At the same time as I watched Kathy being abused in these ways, I watched Ken, who was older than she, be absolved of all responsibilities. In fact, he was coddled like a little baby long into his adolescence. It was as if there had been a landslide and everything that Kathy deserved fell into Ken's pile. Love? Attention? Forgiveness, encouragement, affection, care? Ken got double of everything, and Kathy got nothing.

Each of us have lots of memories of Ken being horrible and Kathy being sweet, but Karen has one memory in particular that sticks out as being especially poignant. Kathy had been put in charge of getting the two youngest children, Donna and me, down for their naps. This wasn't an easy challenge: Donna was still young enough that she cried easily if she wasn't being held, and I was always a light sleeper who could wake at the slightest noise. Kathy, knowing the consequences of failure, took great pains to get us both to sleep.

She hushed and rocked and lullabied until her arms were sore with fatigue, then tucked the babies down and drew the curtains. Then, she tiptoed out of the room. "Could you guys stay as quiet as you can?" she asked Karen and Ken meekly. "I don't want the babies to wake up and disturb Mom."

When Ken heard this, he stood up. He was not one to accept orders, especially not from someone as lowly as Kathy. He had a fire in his eyes. Kathy cringed. Ken picked up a ceramic bowl with oatmeal in it and raised it above his head. Kathy just shook her head silently, pleading with her eyes. Ken laughed: a raucous, mirthless laugh from his gaping throat. He smashed the bowl on the hard floor.

Within seconds, both babies were crying. Kathy stiffened; she clenched her hands into fists. She moved toward the bedroom, but then turned around unexpectedly and looked Ken in the eye. "You..." she stuttered. "You're... you're a *beast*!" she shouted at last. It was the only time Karen heard Kathy raise her voice. She was shaking. She turned back toward the bedroom while Ken stood there dumbfounded. (Kathy did have courage when it was needed but was often so afraid to use it for fear of the consequences that she kept it secretly hidden and continued to act like the meek mild child she was forced to be.)

A smug smile played on Ken's face as our Mom walked into the room with her hand raised, ready to deal out the retribution she thought Kathy deserved. Karen could hear the cold whack of hands on shin and the meaty thud of punches. Kathy didn't scream. She had lost the passion to do that years ago.

Karen tiptoed in to see if Kathy was okay. She was composing herself on the bed. She looked at Karen and smiled awkwardly. "I should have known better," she whispered.

Karen made ready to go to her side when she heard our mother approaching. Mom came up behind her and physically moved Karen out of the room while yelling," she deserved everything she got."

***

I have painted a few small pictures of our life and shown how Kathy got a focused, exaggerated version of the pain we all knew. Like I said, I thought Kathy was oblivious to this pain, or at least oblivious to the fact that there could be anything else. In a way, this made me feel sad, and in another way it seemed like a blessing: was this how God protected her, by making her unaware of the magnitude of her suffering? Well, I was wrong. She was not unaware.

Kathy didn't tell me about her suicide attempt until we were much older. To this day, I am both amazed and ashamed that I didn't know about it. But then, the fact that she kept even that a secret is testament to the way she suffered in silence. She told me one afternoon over tea while we sat in her apartment. I was seventeen, and she was twenty. We had been talking about our past, about Mom and Dad, and the conversation had been very candid. "Nancy," Kathy said suddenly, "I have to get something off my chest."

I pulled my chair in closer and looked her in the eye. I thought I was ready for anything.

"You remember the time when I was fourteen and I had that awful headache? The one that wouldn't go away for two weeks?"

"Yes," I said. "You had a migraine. It was terrible."

"It was no migraine," Kathy said, her gaze dropping to the table. Her fingers fussed with the handle of her teacup. "I took some of Donna's pills, Nancy. A whole bottle of them."

My head swam. Donna had epilepsy. Kathy had taken an entire bottle of epilepsy medication? Why?

"You know how things were with Mom. You know how bad it got. Well, that year was the worst one yet. Mom seemed to never leave me alone. She beat me so often that my old bruises were still purple when she gave me new ones. She beat me, but she also berated me every chance she got. She hissed insults at me every time she passed me in the room. If her intention was to show me that she hated me, well, that worked, but what she also managed to do was make me hate myself."

I took Kathy's hand.

"I hated myself more than a housewife hates a cockroach. I felt like I was disgusting, like I was useless. I remember that I got my period and thought I was dying—and then I realized I wanted to die. I hoped I was dying; I was happy to see all that blood. So, one day, I decided to just do it."

"Kathy," I began, but I didn't know how to continue.

"I was fed up," she said. "It wasn't a dramatic moment. There was no passion, no crying, no melodramatic lighting. I didn't think back over my life. I didn't write a note. I was just so *tired*, Nancy. I was just *done*."

She straightened in her chair. "The easiest thing I could think of was Donna's medicine. It was right there in the bathroom. I left some for her in case she needed it, of course, but I swallowed those pills, one by one, with a glass of water. It was almost boring. I lay down and waited to go to sleep."

"But..." I stammered. "But you woke up."

"I did."

We looked at each other for a long moment. I was too shocked to cry. Kathy took a deep breath and then let out a little laugh.

"I guess epilepsy medicine doesn't work as a suicide drug," she said. "But I woke up with an unbelievable headache. I've never felt anything like it. I couldn't tell anyone why I had it, so I just stayed in my room until it got a bit better.

"I remember that," I said. "Oh, Kathy, if I'd only known…"

"I didn't want to burden you with that knowledge then," she said gently. "It was too much for a child to take. I knew I'd tell you someday, but it wasn't right to tell you then."

That was Kathy: selfless even at the worst of times. I marvelled at her. Here was someone who could survive even her own suicide and still be a good, caring, loving person at the end of it. Where did this goodness come from? How could there be a light shining in such a dark world?

That was when it dawned on me: God was there. It wasn't immediately obvious where He was hiding, but He was there. Kathy was proof. She had been beaten down so far she felt as low as a cockroach, but still the light shone forth from her. She had no reason to be good: there was nothing stopping her from hating the world. Yet, she loved it. She was full of love, perhaps more capable of selfless love than anyone I knew. If there could be light in the life of Kathy, the girl who grew up in a cellar, then God was present. Not just in the high places, in the churches and sunny meadows, but even here, in the lowliest, grimiest holes. God was there amid the rats. He was there at the bottom of that bottle of pills, the ones that left my sister alive.

***

This realization led to a cascade of other realizations. Had God been there for me all along, even when I thought I was alone? I began to take inventory of my life. I thought of the times and places I had felt so low and so dark I couldn't imagine a world with God in it. Was He there? Was I just too young, too blind, and too self-pitying to see Him?

I thought back to the crawl space. That was the place I imagined when I imagined hell. Could God have been there? Concentrating on those memories, I realized there were glimpses of God in them. During those hours spent alone in that dank cellar, something amazing happened each and every time. I remembered it now. At the height of my own panic, just as I'd start to wonder if the oxygen was going to run out or if a monstrous creature was going to attack me from behind, I'd get a feeling of strange calm that would come on quite suddenly. It was almost like a loving hand had reached down and touched my shoulder. It was almost as if a comforting voice had whispered, "Hush, be still; you aren't alone." My heart rate would slow; my breathing would return to normal. The sweat on my brow would abate, and I'd feel my muscles relax. Something or someone was there with me. I knew it, and it was something or someone good. It was God: I could only guess at what that meant, but I knew it to be true. God didn't speak to me, but He communicated with me. He was there in the quiet of the space. He was there in the slow beats of my own heart. He was there even in the sound of the rats' feet scurrying over the woodwork, and He was the white light that had visited me that one frightening day.

I thought back to my time in the hospital when I thought everyone had forsaken me, God included. I realized, combing over those memories, that even then, I had God by my side. His presence had been hard to feel, but in the still of the isolation ward at night, when the only sounds were the nurses' soft-soled footsteps in the hallway and the occasional far-off cry of a sick child, God came to me and stayed with me. How did I know? Again, I could feel Him in the steady thump-thump of my own pulse, in the comforting up-and-down of my own breathing chest. Lying there under the crisp sheets, by the light of a fluorescent lamp the nurses never seemed to turn off, I was able to quell my fear and listen to God. God was there, even in that awful place. If He could find me in that cold, inhuman isolation ward, which had locked doors and a no-visitors policy, He could find me anywhere.

***

God had been with me all along, but I had been a child and hadn't known where to look or what to look for. It took me decades even to begin to figure it out. Finally, in my early adulthood, I was able to take a second look at the album of my life and spot God in all the pictures. God is there, in all our lives, but it's not always easy for us to recognize Him. It's not always easy to read the messages He gives us. I realized, that afternoon with Kathy, that I needed to work on improving my vision, the better to see God.

4
Angels on Earth

A quick review of the events of my childhood makes it clear that it was a sad and scary time, punctuated with moments of trauma. However, a closer look reveals something more: there were rays of joy. There was even, dare I suggest it, evidence of the sacred amid all that dreary profanity. If I look back now, I can see the sacred elements quite easily. It wasn't that easy at the time, which is why I'm so grateful for the gift of hindsight.

A perfect example of this paradox—of the sacred inhabiting the profane, of joy being present in pain—is Christmas. Like any child, I looked forward to Christmas every year. I see now that our Christmas was a very humble one, several steps down from the festive, glittering celebration my own grandchildren enjoy nowadays. Nonetheless, I anticipated it eagerly, and so did my brothers and sisters.

Even though there was little money, Mom worked hard to ensure that we had gifts on Christmas morning, as well as a wonderful holiday meal. Our gifts were modest: Mom would roll up a new coloring book for each of us and stick some crayons in the middle, along with a few other gifts. That was it. But I loved that gift so much! To this day, I still get excited about a new book. Seeing, touching, or smelling one makes me feel alive, and if I hold a new book, I get an amazingly peaceful energy from it, as I am drawn back to those happy Christmas mornings.

In addition to our coloring books, we also received a bread bag half full of Christmas candy. It was just a bread bag, but it seemed to be overflowing with magic. Opening those bags, we'd look around and see smiles on each other's faces. Even Dad would be smiling. I realize now that my parents must have spent money they didn't have on these gifts, and I feel grateful that they tried so hard to give us these wonderful memories. Even if it only happened once a year, they tried, and I remain grateful.

However, Christmas in my family's house was a tale of two holidays: the morning was always joyous, but by late afternoon it had gone downhill. My father, possibly overwhelmed by the emotions of the morning, would start drinking a little earlier and a little harder than usual. By noon he would be drunk, and Mom and he would be screaming at each other. The younger kids could find solace in their coloring books, but as we grew older, it became harder and harder to do so. In this way, Christmas went from being one of the best days of the year to being one of the worst, and this storyline repeated every year.

It's an unfortunate trajectory, but it perfectly illustrates the fact that in my house, even though things were as rotten as they could be, most of the time, there was still the potential for real joy. We were all able to access it somehow, sometimes, however fleetingly. That capacity to glean joy amid hardship is one that served me time and time again.

***

My ability to find joy in the worst scenarios was like a special sense. I like to think I was able to "see angels" on earth where no one else would notice them. When I was a child, I saw these angels and took them for granted. It made perfect sense that they would be there. Why wouldn't they be? Now, as an adult looking back, I see that they were put there by God to comfort and guide me.

Who were these angels? Well, they came in many forms, and none of them had white wings or haloes. For one example, there was the man who owned the farm we lived on when I was small. He was a kind man who lived in the neighboring town. He worked as a pharmacist but liked to try his hand at farming as a hobby. I liked this man and trusted him, though I can't recall his name. I can still see his face in my mind today: he liked to smile. His name has long since vanished from my memory, but his smile remains an indelible image. He worked at the pharmacy in town during the week but came to our house every weekend to work on the adjacent farm, feeding his cattle and tending whatever crops he was experimenting with. He never failed to bring a small box of candy, filled with chocolate and other goodies. Since he owned the local drugstore, he would pick and choose the goodies he thought we'd like best, and he was never wrong.

He never minded that we played in the fields. He saw the joy it brought us and never complained if we trampled his cornrows or upturned his buckets of cattle feed. He would arrive on Sunday morning to find me covered in muck and playing with his equipment and would simply smile and pat me on the head. Contrast that with my father, who totally ignored us regardless of our silliness. I don't know if the pharmacist knew of our personal problems, but his gentle soul blessed me.

During the hay season in the summer months, my siblings and I worked for him. He brought us cases of Pepsi so we could cool off. What a treat that was! We appreciated it even more than the money we made working for him, but the money was certainly helpful, too. He must have known our family could use the extra money, and he gave us this chance to earn it honestly. Since none of us was afraid of hard work and all of us relished the chance to get out of our parents' house, it was a perfect arrangement.

My relationship with this man didn't end when we moved away from the house he owned. Years later, when I was looking to move out on my own and start a life away from my parents, he was the person I turned to for help with my rental deposit. I knew my parents didn't have the money, and I was only a little bit short. I needed the money to make the leap toward freedom and independence. When I approached him, out of the blue one day, to ask for this favor, he didn't even hesitate. Such was his grace and generosity. He handed over the $300 in cash with a warm smile and told me I could pay it back when I was able and that if I wasn't able, then I was to consider it a gift.

Indeed, everything this man gave us was a gift. He brought sunshine with his smile and treats with his hands. As a child, I knew he was special, but today I see the truth: God sent him as an angel on earth to care for us, to offer kindness and comfort to children who never got much of either.

***

There were other angels, I realize now. Down the road a short way was a couple who was consistently friendly and kind to us. The woman, Annie, happened to be my school principal and the eighth grade teacher. Her husband, Bob, was a burly man with a booming voice and invincible smile. While Annie was, by nature, strict and demanding of respect, she was also fair, calm, and kind. Bob, for his part, was never anything other than jolly. You could sense the love between the two of them, and it spilled over onto all of us. They must have known what went on in our house as they went out of their way to be good to us.

They hired us to mow their lawn in the summers. Luckily, it was a huge lawn, bigger than what one kid could mow alone, so we helped each other and split the proceeds. It brought all of us outside, except for Kathy, and it helped us earn money so we could treat ourselves to some of the small luxuries our parents would never be able to afford: a can of pop, a movie theatre ticket, a bottle of nail polish.

Annie and Bob had no children of their own, and they enjoyed the festive bustle of our company. Bob's job was to buy and sell land for logging purposes, and sometimes on Sundays they went out to look at land prospects. My siblings and I took turns going with them. When it was my turn, I was always over the moon because it meant spending a whole day with this happy couple, listening to the radio in their truck, and then—best of all—going out to dinner at a restaurant in town. I remember sitting at the dinner table with them, dressed in my Sunday best. I would be nervous and excited at the same time.

I look back now and see that they, too, were angels on earth: loving people with lots to give. They knew what we lacked in our life at home—namely, money and love—and they graciously gave us both whenever they could. They were almost like surrogate parents, who let us imagine a world where families are happy and people take care of each other. God put them next to us so we could find comfort and peace in our otherwise ugly world.

***

These were some of the angels I encountered on earth. Not every angel, though, has a human form: I found solace and joy in other ways as well. One of the most reliable sources of comfort for me, growing up, was the outdoors. Outside, there were angels all around me in the form of trees, flowers, weeds, wind, and most of all, the animals that shared the countryside with us.

As a child, I was almost always afraid inside my own house. I tiptoed everywhere and kept my eyes open for signs of trouble. But outside? It was a different world, and I was a different person. I was free. I was fearless. I loved the outdoors more than I loved anything else. In the summer, I would close my eyes and walk with my arms stretched out at my sides. I could feel the breeze moving over my skin; it felt like a reassuring caress from a beloved friend. I used to catch frogs and put them in mason jars. I made them my pets if only for a short time. I prided myself on my ability to catch them before they jumped away. I wasn't squeamish about their slime, and I loved their funny little faces. They weren't my only pets. I befriended several more creatures over the years. There was my raccoon, Jimmy, who gleefully ate leftovers right out of my hand and rode around on my foot throughout the day. There was my goat, Billy, whose little bleats sounded to me just like laughter. There was my cat, Cuddles, who was shy with everyone except me, and there was my beloved dog, Toby, a big, muddy mutt who loved to bound through the fields with me every chance he got. The other critters in my special extended family—chipmunks that I convinced to ride in my shirt pocket and bugs that I kept in matchboxes—came and went with the passing days, but I loved each one with all the passion in my little heart. Those animals were put there by God, and whenever I was with them, I felt like I would never be lonely. God had given me these playmates, but they didn't just teach me how to play. They taught me unconditional love—how to give it and how to receive it—which was something my parents were unable to teach me.

In the same creek where I caught those poor frogs, I used to swim every day in the summer. I thought I was the best swimmer, though, in fact, I was just walking in the water, waist-deep, thrashing my arms around ineffectually. I also used to go fishing with my brothers, and I especially loved fishing with Gordon. We always managed to bring some fish home for Mom to cook; she was glad to have the free groceries! We used to play baseball in the pasture beyond our house, and we used cow patties for bases. We would play outside until the sun set nearly every night in the summer. I remember laughing with my siblings until I could laugh no more; we laughed until we hurt.

Outdoors, we were all free and happy. We were children of God, not the children of our parents, and our sisters and brothers were the trees and the foxes and the wind. We found joy; we didn't even have to look for it. Now, looking back, I see that nature was herself one of the angels on earth I knew as a child. It was God's gift to me and to anyone who could appreciate it. Nature offered sweet solace from the pain inside my house and boundless, romping joy to a child who needed it so much.

I want to add a sad note to this memory: while we all frolicked outside with our animal friends, there was one of us who stayed indoors with the anger and the pain. Kathy was never allowed to play outside. Mom made her stay inside to help with chores or as punishment. I have no memories of ever playing with Kathy outside, and she has none herself. I do remember seeing Kathy through the dusty window, watching us while we played. She was never bitter, never self-pitying, and she didn't begrudge us our fun. Still, it pains me now more than I can say to recall that image of her, gazing through the window at a world of joy she could never know.

Why did God offer these gifts, these angels, to the rest of us but not to her? It's a complicated question with no easy answer. Eventually, Kathy would find her solace, but first her suffering would reach a height she hadn't yet imagined.

Nancy Stokkermans

5

When Pain Begets Joy

In our adolescent years, I got lucky: my mom started giving me some positive attention. I still don't know why she did this, but I wasn't going to turn it down. It seems so simple—the occasional smile from her in my direction, the tone of her voice sounding warm instead of icy—but it was enough to change my outlook on life. I felt like the world was in bloom just when my own body was starting to blossom. Kathy, on the other hand, was still being buried in the underworld like Persephone.

As Kathy matured, Mom's attitude toward her only grew worse. She had never had patience for Kathy, who wasn't allowed to make noise like a child, to laugh or cry like a child, or to play like a child. Mom's patience seemed to grow even scarcer as Kathy grew older. Kathy didn't fit in the crawl space anymore, so Mom resorted to hitting her harder and more frequently and to hurling ever more scathing insults. Kathy seemed to take it all in stride, but I know now (and I sensed even then) that it was killing her.

While I was able to start looking out at the world in a positive, open way, seeing what it had to offer me, Kathy was able only to peer at it suspiciously, desperately. So, it is no surprise that she took the first opportunity for escape that she could find. Unfortunately, it came in the form of a guy.

I call him simply "a guy" because he could have been anyone. I don't think Kathy was waiting for a knight in shining armour. She knew better than to expect that. She was merely waiting for someone, anyone, to come along and distract her from the torment of her life, and it happened to be this person, this guy, whose name I don't even remember. I'm sure Kathy remembers it, though.

He was nineteen; Kathy was fifteen. He asked Kathy to go on a camping trip with him, and my parents raised no argument against it. Surely, they were happy to get rid of her, and she was happy to be got rid of. Looking back (now that I have been a parent myself), my mind reels that they would let her go on this trip with this boy. He was older than she; she was just a child, a virgin with no experience of any kind at all, let alone sexual experience. She did not know how to protect herself; no one had ever showed her. How could they send her off like this, a lamb to the slaughter?

Kathy very much enjoyed her time with this boy and immediately fell in love with him. She loved his attention and his tender words. It seemed like a fairy tale come true: someone loved her and wanted her just the way she was. All of these tender feelings and words led to Kathy's first sexual experience, one she was neither prepared for nor fully understood. However, she learned quickly because the experience came with a lot of pain physically and emotionally. She came home from the camping trip with visible bruises on the outside and invisible ones on the inside. What's more, she learned she was pregnant from the experience. She had no choice but to tell my parents.

What would you do if you learned your daughter was pregnant? The answer seems like a no-brainer: you would console her, you would help her, you would take her to the appropriate medical and counseling centers and would vow, with your fist in the air, to avenge the injustice. You would take her in your arms and hold her. You would weep into her hair that you are sorry, you are sorry, you are sorry. I have daughters. I know what I would do.

I have talked enough about my parents that by now it will come as no surprise that they reacted with nothing but anger and scorn. "You stupid slut!" my mother yelled. "How do you expect me to deal with this? How could you do this to me?"

"I didn't do it, Mom; it was done to me! I didn't even know what was happening until it was too late," Kathy pleaded in vain.

"You will take responsibility for this yourself, you little whore," my mother seethed. "You act like a slut, you pay the price."

Rather than having the boy arrested for sexual assault on a minor, my parents ridiculed Kathy and ramped up their efforts to make her life hell. She was now referred to only as "Slut" and "Whore," never by her name. My mother mocked her for her stupidity (as though getting pregnant from ignorance was something she could control) and took every chance to remind her of the torment that awaited her. "I hope this baby creates so much pain that you cannot stand it."

Kathy suffered terrible morning sickness, but naturally she had to keep that a secret and found no comfort from it. To make matters worse, the father of the baby—the man Kathy loved—disappeared as soon as he found out Kathy was pregnant, never to be seen again. Kathy cried herself to sleep every night; I heard her. I also heard her pray to God to let her keep the baby.

Because Kathy was a minor, she had no say in the custody of the baby. Mom and Dad had the legal right to decide the baby's fate. I don't know what they wanted in their own hearts, but as soon as Mom heard that Kathy wanted to keep the baby, she announced that it would be given up for adoption. Kathy's tears when she heard this were the deepest she ever cried. I was still a naïve child, and I held out hope that my parents would change their minds. I looked at Kathy's growing belly, and my heart leapt at the idea of the tiny person growing in there. I wanted a baby so much, and I was secretly grateful to Kathy for bringing us one. While I childishly fantasized about having a baby in the house, Kathy wept in pure despair at the thought of giving her precious child to a stranger.

Kathy had to quit school due to her pregnancy, so she helped out around the house as much as possible. Even though she was big, uncomfortable, hot, and exhausted, she was still a tremendous help to my parents. Did they appreciate it? Of course not. They taunted and ridiculed her, day in and day out. I remember the final months of Kathy's pregnancy as being a particularly cruel and awful time for her.

***

One day in early March, the ninth to be exact, Kathy's labor began. She didn't mention it at first. She was accustomed to pain and so was able to endure the early hours of labor without making a sound. Finally, when the contractions were long and strong, she told me what was happening. There were tears in her eyes when she told me.

"Nancy, the baby's coming," she said, her breaths slow and measured.

"Now? Today?" I squealed. My heart rate shot up. I was terrified and excited at once.

"I think so," Kathy said, and leaned over the dresser in her bedroom to endure a contraction. I watched her deal with the pain. I had heard about childbirth, and I had seen depictions of it in movies. Why wasn't Kathy screaming and ripping her hair out? Why wasn't she causing a ridiculous scene? Why weren't we rushing to the hospital in an ambulance? Kathy was amazing: she was so young and so scared, yet here she was, bearing the world's most notorious pain with the grace and strength of a saint. I marvelled at her.

"I'll tell Mom and Dad," I said breathlessly and ran to the kitchen to get them.

Lord, Did You Cry With Me When Mommy Hit Me?

When I announced, "The baby is coming! Hurry! Do something!" my dad only gave an insolent grunt. He had just opened a beer; now he would have to abandon it or drink it too quickly. My mother's lips grew thin, and she stormed to Kathy's bedroom. "Get your things," she snapped. "Meet us in the car."

Everything seemed to go in slow motion from then on. Why wasn't anyone but me dashing about? While I gathered Kathy's boots and her suitcase, a myriad of thoughts streamed through my mind: Why all the tears? It can't hurt that much! What is she afraid of? As confused as I was, I could not help but yell at Mom and Dad to get moving. This was an emergency!

As Kathy huddled in the back of the car, shaking from the cold, her panicked stare completely alarmed me. I held her hand and whispered, 'I will pray for you." Her tears began to fall as another pain held her in its grip. I wanted to stay with her, by Mom ordered me, "Close the door and get in the house before you freeze to death!"

I closed the door, and the car disappeared into the blinding snow. Standing among the swirling snowflakes, I begged God to take care of my family.

Kathy was terrified of what was to come. She knew Dad could barely see out the windshield as he tried to keep the car on the road. The wind seemed to blow right through the outer shell of the car and straight through her. She shook; she cried. Other than that, all was silent. No one spoke. Neither parent attempted to console her, but then, Kathy really didn't expect any comfort, just punishment.

As Kathy curled her body into the fetal position with the hope of easing some of the pain she realized that moisture was leaking down her legs. Her panic increased in accompaniment with her sobs. She was having her baby and was terrified. Dad sped up, understanding from the crescendo of Kathy's crying that time is running out. The snowstorm was his enemy, and he must stand and fight even if he is still angry with his daughter.

Mom sat absolutely quietly, not a sound came from her. What was she thinking? Was she scared, too?

The car stopped. Kathy lifted her head and saw the lights from the hospital emergency room. Hope filled her heart for one heartbeat as the car door opened and Dad pulled her out. To her shock, he drove away, leaving her standing in the snow. Everything was silent once more. She would have to find her own way into the hospital and into helping hands.

To this day, I am stunned that my parents left their child to endure such pain and emotional trauma alone. I am even more amazed that Kathy was able to endure it. I stand in awe of her. She endured this impossible experience with dignity and courage. I have been proud of her many times in my life, but this one stands out as a pivotal triumph.

In the hospital that night, Kathy met an angel here on earth. Her attending nurse was a nondescript young woman—average size, hair in a practical bun, a plain but gentle face—but she played a role that may have saved my sister's sanity. She stayed with Kathy the entire night as her labor wore on and racked her body. She held Kathy close and spoke softly, encouraging her with loving words. At times, Kathy wondered if she was dreaming this woman. She was like the mother Kathy never had. This nurse was sent by God—I know it now—to stand in for the absent mother in Kathy's life and to offer the love that every woman needs as she gives birth.

During the deepest part of the night, when yesterday's sunset is as far away as tomorrow's sunrise, a beautiful, healthy baby entered our world. Kathy loved her little girl instantly. In fact, she had fallen in love long before delivery. She begged to be allowed to hold her, but orders had been given to the nurses that Kathy was not to see or hold her baby. However, the wonderful nurse who had helped her through the night went against my parents' wishes and let Kathy hold her baby. Kathy says it was as though the universe opened up and swallowed her whole. She had never felt a love like that, could never have been prepared for it. It felt like she had been washed away by a tidal wave, like she was drowning under an ocean of crushing, crashing love.

With tears of joy and tears of pain rolling down her face, Kathy reluctantly handed the baby back to the nurse, knowing it was the last time she would ever hold her dear baby.

***

I lay awake in my bed, squirming with nervousness and anticipation. I had heard my parents come home and knew that Kathy was out there somewhere on the verge of meeting her baby. I knew she would have to give the baby up—my parents had made that very clear—but I couldn't help myself: I was exploding with joy. A little niece or nephew! I already felt the deepest love for this little soul.

I imagined Kathy in her hospital bed, suffering. Was she alone? Was she afraid? How I wished I could be with her! I would put my hand on her forehead. I would stroke her big belly. I would whisper encouragement in her ear. I scorned my parents for leaving her all alone and prayed that she had someone to hold her hand. I didn't know about the nurse, but indeed my prayer was being answered in real time.

I prayed that Kathy would be okay. People died in childbirth, didn't they? It happened in stories I had read. I tried not to think of blood, of infection, of puerperal fever, a name that frightened me. I prayed that she'd be okay, but at the same time I just *knew* she'd be okay. Somehow, God was communicating that to me. He was telling me, without words or obvious signs, that He would protect her. I also prayed (possibly with even more fervour) that we could keep her baby. My parents seemed to make a hobby of saying "no" to us when we asked for something, and this one was surely the biggest "no" of all. I prayed nonetheless. I felt like the baby already belonged to us, had belonged to us for nine months.

In the morning, I woke up to the sound of the phone ringing. I shot up like a firecracker and tore down the hall to eavesdrop.

"Yes, that's right," my mother said into the phone. Her mood was inscrutable. "Yes, we would." There was a pause. My mother's face showed no emotion, and she held the phone with a firm hand.

Then her expression changed. Her eyes softened with tears, and her voice broke when next she spoke. "A little girl," she said and put the phone to her chest. She looked at me, her lip trembling, and then composed herself.

That was it. I had a niece! My heart swelled with joy. I thought I'd burst. I clamped my hands over my mouth to hide my wild smile.

"Thank you," my mother said into the phone and hung up. She was impassive. Businesslike. Free of emotion. But I had seen her face when she heard the news, and I knew what she felt in her heart. It was all I could do to hold in my squeals of excitement.

I didn't go with them to the hospital, but I heard about it later. They had arrived on the maternity floor and gone straight to the nursery to see the baby. The nurses, who knew about their plans to put the baby up for adoption, put on poker faces as they led them down the hall. Normally, they would offer congratulations and hand the baby over gleefully to its loving grandparents, but this time everything was formal and rigid. A nurse gave the baby to my father, and he held it awkwardly in his big arms. He stared down into the little baby's otherworldly eyes. She let out a gentle peep. Her smell was intoxicating, the smell of life.

Then, that big, hard man, whose jaw had been set in a frown for a decade, collapsed into a laugh. He laughed softly but surely, his eyes wide with wonder at the perfect person in his arms. His laughter complemented his tears, and it was obvious to everyone in the room that he had melted. He didn't even have to say it, but he said it: "We're keeping her. She's part of our family."

There was much celebrating, then, in the hallway outside the little nursery. My mother and father embraced. They even embraced the nurses. What joy rang out! Meanwhile, alone in her ward room, Kathy sobbed, unaware of the change of plans, bereft at the loss of her daughter. She told me later that her sorrow then was tantamount to the joy she'd felt at holding her baby for the first time. It was nearly an hour before anyone told her the news.

***

A week later, Kathy was released from hospital and brought her beautiful little miracle with her. Her name was Cindy. Cindy, beautiful Cindy! Her name sounded to me like tinkling bells. I adored her; we all adored her. It was as though our entire family had undergone an emotional makeover; we were nearly unrecognizable!

However, within a few days, Mom was back to her usual disposition, especially with regard to Kathy. She was still over the moon about the baby but refused to let Kathy enjoy the honeymoon phase with her little newborn. When Kathy was only nine days postpartum, Mom told her she had to get a job, and that she would start the next morning. She had arranged for Kathy to work the line at a local factory, taking the 3pm–11pm shift. This way, Kathy could work all day and take care of the baby all night because Mom refused to get up with the baby in the night. She also made Kathy do all the laundry, her own and the baby's. Poor Kathy would go to work, where she had to sit on a rubber donut because she was still so sore from the birth, and come home exhausted, only to have a newborn baby to assume the care of. Kathy was still bleeding from the birth herself and was using cloth diapers on Cindy (disposables were still relatively new and too expensive), so there was a lot of laundry to do. On top of that, we didn't have a washing machine, so Kathy had to scrub the blood and feces out of the laundry with a washboard, then hang them on a clothesline to dry—in the winter. She would finish the laundry and then collapse into bed with the baby, only to sleep wretchedly on and off until her shift that afternoon. For poor Kathy, reality came crashing down on her in short order. For the rest of us, though, Cindy was a dream come true, and we felt like we were dancing with an angel.

I knew it as soon as I laid eyes on her: Cindy was my soul mate. I knew we would have a special bond that would last all of our lives. I wasn't wrong; Cindy and I still have an amazing bond. She is part of my heart and soul, and I love her with every ounce of who I am. I will always be grateful to Kathy for giving me—and the world—the amazing gift of our Cindy.

6

The Catalyst

I had been taken aback, when Cindy arrived home by the impossible feeling of knowing with absolute certainty that I was bonded to her in a way that was bigger than anything the words "aunt" or "niece" could explain. It made me curious: how does this kind of bond work? Could I feel it with anyone else? Why did I have it with Cindy? Had I met her in some other world before either of us was born? Had we met in a parallel universe or in another life? I felt silly for thinking these thoughts, but at the same time I couldn't shake them. The possibilities excited and scared me at the same time, but one thing was for sure: Cindy was my soul mate. I knew her inside and out as soon as I met her, and my love for her was the most constant thing I'd ever felt. It was the surest thing I knew. As many questions as this rose for me, in some ways it felt like an answer in itself. It felt like a *yes*, a giant, booming *YES*, resounding from the voice of heaven. Whatever the question was, the answer was *yes*, and whatever this strange emotion was, it made me feel closer to God.

***

After Cindy's birth, our entire household underwent a strange but wonderful transformation. The chaos and stress that had once haunted our normal routine seemed to diminish, all because of this little person with a round blonde head and laughing eyes. Family dinners were suddenly festive events instead of fear-laden ones: everyone talked, laughed, and told stories. They were characterized by giggles instead of tears. Mom and Dad chatted about the progress of the vegetable gardens while we children laughed and teased each other about anything we could think of. Was this really the family I grew up in? Was this the same dinner table where my mother used to cry, where my siblings and I used to tremble in fear lest she explode in rage again? All aspects of our home seemed calmer now. It was strange but wonderful.

Now that our family was actually experiencing joy, the physical abuse stopped. I thank God for that miracle, even now. Life was better in so many ways: I had Cindy, I was playing lots of sports, and I was generally enjoying myself. What's more, my mother had begun to show me that she cared. Whereas in the past she had all but ignored me, now she asked me about my assignments, my grades, and how the other students were treating me. My mom was becoming my friend. We started taking long walks together, taking turns pushing Cindy's buggy while dodging the many potholes. I remember one walk in particular. The day was hot, and we meandered down to the creek where we sat with our feet dangling in the cool water.

Mom was quiet for a while. Then she glanced over at the buggy where Cindy was napping. "Things really have brightened up around here since Cindy came along," she said dreamily. "Are you happy she's here?"

"Of course, Mom," I gushed. I was thrilled to be able to talk about Cindy, the love of my life. "Cindy is my niece, my baby sister, and my best friend, all in one. She has given us all so much already," I said.

Mom smiled. She gripped my hand and gave it a squeeze. Neither of us said another word, but we didn't have to. We both felt grateful to Cindy for bringing us closer to each other. I revelled in that moment: here was my mom, asking to hear my thoughts, sitting beside me in peace. I could feel her love just as I could feel the cool water splashing against my feet. I wasn't sure how long her love would last, but I wanted to get as much of it as I could.

***

It was a different story between my father and me. He continued to ignore me as if I was just another mouth to feed and not a daughter who needed love. Of course, it hurt to think that my father didn't love me, but I shut that pain out and focused on the love of Cindy and my mom. This made me feel better, but what was it about my dad? It seemed that nothing could soften his hard heart.

Well, almost nothing. I remember watching him with Cindy, and it was like he was a different person altogether. He would play with her, really play with her, when he never would have wasted his time playing with any of us. His eyes lit up when he looked at Cindy, and he thought nothing of making a complete fool of himself for her sake. He would get down on all fours and imitate a cow, complete with mooing sounds. He would put her on his shoulders and zip around the house, making helicopter noises. He was silly with her, and when he was silly, he was happy, almost like he was a child himself. I don't think he knew I was watching him when he did this. Had he known, he probably would have stopped. What was it about Cindy, then? She was the only thing on earth that could ignite the fire in this man's heart. The only times I ever heard him laugh were when he was playing with Cindy.

I watched them play together and my heart soared. Strangely enough, it never occurred to me to feel jealous. Here was my father, who never had more than a hostile grunt for me, giving himself freely and joyously to Cindy. He was giving her everything he should have given me: love, attention, affection, and time. He was my father, and she was getting what rightfully should have been mine. So, why was I not upset?

I think the answer is that I identified so fully with Cindy that her joy was my joy. If she was happy, so was I, even if the situation was complicated. Watching her play with my dad, I was able to absorb some of that joy, some of that love, as though it was channelling right through Cindy and into me. I knew she would share that joy with me if she could, and so I felt no resentment toward her for experiencing it. In a way, I think I was living vicariously through her. She was my proxy, and I was able to imagine being loved by my father through her. Maybe it wasn't the perfect arrangement, but it was better than nothing, which is what I was used to.

In fact, I even felt happy for my father. I had never seen him like this, and I realized that he probably wished he could have been kinder to us. There was something holding him back all his life—an anxiety, a sadness, an unnamed darkness. I was glad that he was finally able to taste a little bit of unfettered joy. If it was not directed at me, so what? It was a miracle that he was experiencing it at all.

Dad was still his introverted self most of the time, and he remained indifferent to the rest of us. However, I did see that he was a little softer around the edges. It may have been a very subtle difference, but I noticed it. He was gentler with my mom, less inclined to start or continue a fight. I saw him touch her more; he was more generous with his physical affection. While he ignored my siblings and me most of the time, his very posture seemed more relaxed, and he no longer seemed to cast the malignant shadow we were all so used to. This got me thinking: all my life I had prayed to God to "fix" my parents. I had figured God would do this in an obvious way, but I never saw any evidence of it. I had prayed for my dad to be kind to me, to love me, to pay attention to me. My dad never did any of those things, so I figured God had ignored my prayers.

But maybe I was looking in the wrong places for the answers to my prayers. Here, right in front of me, was one such answer: I was staring right at it. My dad was able to love, possibly for the first time in his life. He was happy, and the whole family was benefitting from it. I made the connection: God had answered my prayer by giving us Cindy. Cindy was the catalyst that transformed both of my parents into loving people at last. It seems so clear to me now, decades later, but at the time it took some mental gymnastics to see that God had been listening, after all.

God *is* paying attention, I learned, but it only works if I'm paying attention too.

***

Our household had settled into a new, comfortable order. We were all happier, but that doesn't mean things were perfect. I don't want to give a false impression: Cindy's birth had brought joy to all of us, but there were so many problems running so deep in my family that nothing could be a cure-all, not even Cindy. I learned that miracles do happen but that even miracles are complicated. God does not simply wave a magic wand. We have to work *with* His miracles; we have to do our share of the work.

Mom and Kathy were getting along better, but there was still some tension underlying their relationship. For example, Mom made Kathy wake up in the night to feed and care for Cindy even though Kathy had to be up at the crack of dawn every day to work a hard shift at the factory. Kathy was functioning on very little sleep, but Mom showed no mercy: Kathy would care for Cindy at night, case closed. At the time, I wondered if Mom was being fair. Was she punishing Kathy for getting pregnant in the first place, or was she trying to teach her some responsibility? Was she being cruel, or was she giving Kathy a gift? Looking back, I think it was a bit of both.

Another problem that underlay our mostly happy home life can be summed up with one word: Ken. Our oldest brother had always been favored by Mom, and we had learned to live with it. It was unfair: she let him get away with everything but punished Kathy for the slightest infractions. She showed Ken love when all he gave back was hostility and spite. I always knew Ken was disturbed, but one morning he showed me just how dangerous he could be. I was playing with Cindy on the living room floor, and Ken was ranting around the house in one of his moods. We were all very familiar with Ken's "moods," during which he'd swear and curse and spew out violent, hateful, awful comments, directed at anyone and everyone. Usually, we tried to ignore him. On this morning, though, I couldn't stand it. Cindy, as pure and innocent as a little sparrow, was sitting right in front of him, soaking it all in. I hated the idea that he could poison her with his awful words, with his unprovoked rage. So, I called him on it. I told him what I thought of his attitude, and I told him to stop.

Ken boiled over. He ran into the other room and grabbed one of my father's shotguns. He loaded it in front of me. He aimed it at my head.

Ken was standing three feet away from me. He was frothing at the mouth. His eyes were like an animal's. I knew he was capable of anything. "I'm going to fucking kill you!" he seethed.

I was stunned at first. I froze. Then, the adrenaline kicked in, and I swooped Cindy from her walker and ran with her. I moved faster than I ever have in my life. I ran outside until I was far away from the house, and I stood there in the afternoon drizzle, holding Cindy close to my heart. My chest was heaving, gasping for breath, but she was fine: oblivious of what was transpiring, happy simply to be in my arms. I kissed her wet head, grateful that I'd managed to get her out of there, away from that monster. That's what Ken was: a monster.

***

In the days following that incident, I tried to forget about it. I tried to ignore the negative aspects of my home life and focus on the happier, more positive ones. These had been wonderful days, and I didn't want them to end. I didn't want to admit that things could be less than perfect, even though Ken had made that pretty obvious. Still, for the first time in my life, it felt like life was good. With Cindy in my life, I knew true joy. With Cindy in my life, I woke up smiling and felt like anything was possible. Was this how life was going to be from now on, or was it too good to be true? Was this happiness like a house of cards, beautiful but fatally fragile?

Then, one morning, my fears came true. The house of cards came fluttering down. Kathy announced that she was leaving, and she was taking Cindy with her.

Why? How could she do this? I couldn't even think straight when I heard the news. I ran to my room, stumbling through the blur of my tears. Oh God, I prayed, why would you tease me like this: show me true joy only to rip it away from me again? I wept so bitterly I thought I'd drown. My sobs were deep and racked my body. When I was able to pause for breath, I heard a timid knock on my door.

"Nancy? It's Kathy."

"Go away. I don't even want to see you right now!" I shouted. My sadness was mixing with anger, though I wasn't even sure who to be angry at. Kathy? My parents? God?

"Nancy, listen to me. I need to tell you why I'm doing this."

I slowly got up and opened the door. Kathy's face was tear-streaked, just like mine. She looked apologetic but determined. I let her in, and we sat down together on the bed.

"You know how much I love my daughter," Kathy began. I nodded. I loved her daughter, too. "And you know how hard it was for me, growing up in this house. Nancy, even if things seem happier now, I don't want to expose Cindy to any of the stuff I went through. Ever."

I glowered at Kathy, still unwilling to give up my anger. "What about me?" I demanded. "Cindy is my niece. Not only that, she's my best friend! I don't want to live without her!" It was all I could do to contain my sobs.

"I know, Nancy. I know." Kathy sighed deeply and straightened her shoulders. "I'm sorry that this is going to hurt everyone, even Cindy, at first. But I have to do right by her. I have to. And I know that this is not the place for us. If you think about it, you know it, too."

It was obvious that Kathy had thought this through and wasn't going to change her mind. I recalled the bruises and blows she'd received at my mother's hands over the years. I recalled the way her spirit had been all but extinguished by the relentless abuse and hate. I admitted it to myself: Kathy was right. She had to get out of here, and she had to take Cindy with her. It was her way of saving them both.

"I understand," I said softly. It was all I could say. Kathy opened her arms, and I fell into them.

"There's one more thing," she said, releasing our embrace.

"What is it?" I asked.

"It might not seem so big, but it's big to me. Mom and Dad have started making Cindy call them 'Mom' and 'Dad' — you know, instead of 'Grandma' and 'Grandpa.'"

"So?"

"So, it's like they're trying to take her away from me, slowly but surely. Next they'll have her calling me 'Kathy.' Well, it's not right. Cindy is my daughter, not theirs." Kathy's voice broke up, and her lip trembled. "Being her mother is the best thing I've ever done. I'm good at it, Nancy. I'm a good mother, and I'm not going to let them take that away from me."

I've never seen Kathy look braver. In that moment, I was in awe of her: here was someone who had endured unspeakable abuse, but instead of being weakened by it, she was empowered. I would mourn the loss of my beloved Cindy, but I gave Kathy my blessing.

***

After Kathy and Cindy left, I really noticed the cracks and flaws in what had seemed like a perfect family portrait. However, I also realized that things didn't have to be so black and white. Maybe life could still be good without Cindy in the home. Maybe the miracles that God had wrought by bringing her to us in the first place could be sustained. I vowed to hold some of Cindy's joy in my heart, day by day. I vowed to remember the lessons she had taught me about unconditional love and uncomplicated joy.

Although things were gloomier in the house without Cindy's smile to brighten the rooms, we all tried to maintain the atmosphere she had helped us create. My mother and I strove to work on our relationship, and even my father seemed lighter in spirit. Ken was still a brooding, nasty ogre, but we were all able to let his insults roll off our backs. I decided to hold onto the optimism and joy she had helped me discover. I got more involved in sports at school and found that I was a natural athlete. All that practice as a tomboy had paid off. I was more outgoing socially, and started meeting boys. I was new at dating, so I refused most of their offers, but when a young man named Frank came along, there was something about him that made me say "yes." Maybe it was his bright blue eyes or his sunny blond hair. Maybe it was his wonderfully silly smile. Whatever it was, something inside of me woke up when I met him, and we started dating right away.

My life had certainly changed a lot in a few short months. I had gone from the peaks of happiness—welcoming Cindy into my life—to the depths of sadness—losing her. I had learned not only how to experience joy but also how to hold onto it. I had learned how to recognize that God was listening to me:

I learned the codes He uses and the subtle ways He answers prayers. I was becoming more and more attuned to the presence of God in my life. As my relationship with God grew and burgeoned, my relationship with Frank grew, too. In time, he became not just my boyfriend but my husband-to-be.

7
Young Love

Frank and I had a picture-perfect romance from the beginning. We went out every weekend. Roller-skating, fishing, picnicking, movies, and pizza were all part of the fun. As far as my teenage heart was concerned, I was totally in love with Frank. Long before he proposed, I would imagine our wedding, our honeymoon, our children, our pets. I would imagine our house in luscious detail, picturing everything from the tablecloths to the curtains to the wind chimes on the porch. We clicked perfectly, Frank and I, and we enjoyed talking about the future, so I had a hunch that he was thinking of the same things I was. However, we also had lots of arguments. I lacked good role models, growing up with two parents incapable of showing love or even civility to each other, so when Frank and I fought, I fought badly. I screeched and wailed. I accused and defended. I sulked. These were the only techniques I knew! I was an insecure teenager, and this was my first relationship. I knew I would have to learn how to fight like a grown-up, and I vowed to figure out how. Frank, for his part, was patient and understanding. He knew how to diffuse a fight, to make me laugh, and to make me feel loved and special. Since he was young, too, though, there were awkward kinks to work out as we navigated this new path together.

Frank came from a family that dictated his choices in life. They were dyed-in-the-wool farmers of Dutch stock, and they had strict protocols and unwavering priorities. This legacy had its benefits. For example, Frank was not afraid of hard work and always made sure his work got done. Further, he loved the work he did. Farming was in his blood. Yet, it also had its drawbacks. Any system so inflexible is bound to grate against the will of a young man (and especially of his willful bride-to-be).

Frank's family was Roman Catholic. They expected everyone in the family to attend weekly Mass unless sickness or work kept them away. Interested in the teachings of the Church and pleased to be considered family, I accepted this expectation. I was curious about how organized religion worked and eager for the chance to be part of any congregation. I wasn't picky about which one. After all, it seemed to me that all churches lead to God, and I felt that God and I were good friends. He wouldn't care which church I wandered into, just that I was there.

I didn't think there was anything terribly controversial about going to church with my future in-laws, but my father seemed to go into a darker mood on Sunday mornings when I'd get dressed in my best. When I finally asked him about it, he admitted that Frank's Catholicism bothered him.

"You know it's a lot of bullshit," he grunted, his eyes down.

"What is, Dad?"

"The church. The pope. The water into wine. You really believe that's the body of Christ they have stored away in that tabernacle? Like a Tupperware container?" Dad was getting his ire up.

"I don't know, Dad. I'm there to find out what I believe, I guess, but I appreciate the symbols they use to describe the mystery of God. And I appreciate that everyone there is seeking God."

"Well, it's nonsense, all of it." Dad opened a beer and took a long, insolent swig.

"What is it about the Catholic church you don't like?" I asked.

"Well, for starters, everything," he said. "And it's not just the Catholics. It's the Anglicans, the Protestants, the Presbyterians; it's the Muslims and the Jews and the Buddhists and the Sikhs. It's the Seventh-Day-Adventists and the Mormons with their little penguin suits."

"You hate religion?" I asked. I knew he hated it when my mom read the *Bible*, but I was just now beginning to see the extent of his scorn.

"I hate anything that dupes people into believing there's a loving God who's going to watch out for them. I hate anything that pulls the wool over so many people's eyes, that tricks them into thinking there are answers, that there's anything out there but a vast, indifferent chaos. Religion is a game for idiots, and I don't want my daughter playing it." He finished his beer with one long pull.

I didn't know what to make of that conversation with my dad. I had to empathize. He had had a horrible life; not much had happened to convince him of a loving God. By the same token, he had never sought evidence of such a God. He had only wallowed in his tragedies and drowned his soul in sorrows. He had chosen atheism because it provided an intellectual framework for his cynical grief and seemed to legitimize it for him. I could see why this sad, wounded man felt the way he did, but I didn't have to inherit his attitude. I knew God was real. I had always known it, and I would seek God by whatever means were available to me. The Catholic Church was available to me now, It was welcoming me inside its doors. I would enter.

***

Frank and I decided that I should be baptized—first things first. After that, I attended Mass every Sunday with Frank and his family, and we took marriage preparation classes with the priest. I absorbed as much as I could from the whole experience, opening my heart and mind to everything I heard. The priest seemed wise. His homilies were eloquent and often inspirational, and he seemed to have a lot of useful marriage advice though he had, of course, never been married himself. I sang hymns from the hymn books, followed along with the readings, and did my best to be a picture-perfect Catholic. I really wanted things to work out between me and this particular version of God.

As my wedding day approached, I felt nothing but happy anticipation. I had none of the nerves you hear about, no cold feet. I was thrilled to be marrying Frank, the love of my life, and I was equally thrilled to be marrying him in God's house. I didn't care so much about my dress, or the flowers, or the weather. There were only two things I needed on that day: Frank and God.

As it happened, my wedding day was perfect by any standards, not just my own. The sun shone warm but not too bright as playful clouds dotted the blue sky. The air was just warm enough that no one shivered and just cool enough that no one had to worry about perspiration, either. The breeze blew through my hair, and I felt the love of God in its soft caress. I had everything I wanted, and I was smart enough to know it: I felt overwhelmed with gratitude that day. *Thank you, God*, I whispered to the shining sun. "Thank you, Frank," I whispered to my new husband.

***

My husband and I moved into a new house. Frank had helped build it, and it was connected to the farm he owned with his brother. I was surrounded on all sides by my husband's life: his job, his family, and his dreams. At the time, we were all happy with the arrangements. It was a little oppressive if I stopped to think about it, but I didn't stop to think about it much. I was too euphoric, too caught up in the joys of being a newlywed.

Lord, Did You Cry With Me When Mommy Hit Me?

Marriage was wonderful, and I was so in love. I went to work at a barley plant research plant each day, walking on air, and hurried home so I could be with my husband. I missed him when we were apart even if it was only for the length of a shift. My need for his attention and his love grew stronger every day. I took care of him and nurtured him the way I had always wanted someone to nurture me. I loved being a wife. I wanted the dream life: a husband, children, pets, a white picket fence, and all the trimmings. I wanted a life that was nothing like the life I came from.

I needed to make things right, to undo my past. I was not going to be like my parents, for one thing. I was going to honor my spouse. I was going to love my children. Not only that, I was going to make sure my husband and children *knew* how much I loved them.

***

I remember with perfect clarity the day I took the home pregnancy test. How my hands shook as I pried it out of its box! I was home alone. Frank was out in the fields. I already knew I was pregnant. God had told me so. Besides, I could feel it in the swirl of mild nausea that accompanied each morning, but I wanted proof so I'd have something to show to Frank. I picked up the store-bought test and quickly read the instructions, skimming over everything except the part about how long you're supposed to wait. Three minutes? Three minutes is an eternity when the fate of your future is on the line. Still, I followed the directions, obedient and hopeful. I left the bathroom and paced around, as nervous as a mouse. I counted to one hundred and eighty in my head. I went back in and glanced at the little plastic stick lying on the bathroom sink. There they were, plain as day: two blue lines.

Two blue lines: they seem so innocuous, so meaningless, and so arbitrary. They just sit there like an equals sign, blue on white. They are merely the result of a simple chemical reaction, but the sight of them has set so many hearts afire, has changed the course of so many lives. There they were, my two blue lines, the equals sign between my present and my future. I was going to be a mother. It was going to come true.

Frank was elated when I told him, as I knew he would be. We had been talking about "making some little Stokkermans," and we had officially begun trying just a few weeks earlier. It was one of God's sweet gifts that we had success on our first attempt, and I thanked God heartily in my prayers every night. I was not only thrilled at the idea of being pregnant, but also I was one of those women who enjoy the physical reality of being pregnant. Sure, I could do without the morning sickness and the heartburn, but most of my symptoms were relatively mild. Truth be told, I felt better than I ever had before. In my diary at the time, I called pregnancy "an inspiring ecstasy that fills my heart and soul each day." I was full of energy, full of optimism, full of life. My hair was thicker than normal. My skin was clearer than normal. My eyes were brighter than normal. Though I found that I could cry at the drop of a hat, most of the time I cried happy tears. I rubbed my belly all day long, even before it started to grow—but once it started, it really grew.

My belly was huge, and my baby was active. Once it started kicking, I felt like I was hosting a soccer match. Even my doctor thought this was unusual. I was bigger than he expected, and my baby seemed more active than what most women reported. He decided to order an ultrasound—these weren't routine at the time—because he thought something might be wrong. For my part, I knew nothing was wrong. I had talked with God about my pregnancy so many times and had felt nothing but reassurance that everything was fine. My doctor wanted to rule out polyhydramnios, a condition involving an excess of amniotic fluid, and I was happy to consent to the ultrasound. It would give me a sneak peak at my little peanut.

Before the ultrasound, I had asked my doctor if it were possible that I could be having twins. That would explain all the movement as well as my extra-large size, I reasoned. He quickly dismissed the idea, however. He had picked up only one heartbeat with the fetoscope. Indeed, when I went for the ultrasound, I learned that there was only one baby.

I was also happy to learn that I didn't have polyhydramnios or any other complication. However, at my next appointment, the doctor and I were both astonished to realize that my belly had grown more than double the amount that it should have in that time, and I asked him to order another ultrasound. He reluctantly agreed. The previous one had shown no abnormalities, but it hadn't explained anything, either.

The appointment was scheduled for the following week. I picked up my mom so she could come with me. This pregnancy had brought my mother and me closer together. She was interested in hearing all the details, and she came with me to every appointment. I was grateful for this sudden friendship with her though unsure about how long it would last. Part of me wanted to stay pregnant forever just so I could sustain the relationship! That day, we drove to my appointment under a sunny sky. "What do you think the test will show?" my mother asked.

"I don't know what I'm expecting to see, Mom," I admitted. "The last test didn't show anything, and the doctor is sure there's nothing to see. But I have a feeling..."

"A feeling about what?"

"A feeling about twins." I smiled wryly at my mom.

"But there's only one baby there. You heard the heartbeat. You even saw it with your own eyes!"

"I know, I know. It's crazy! But I feel like God has been giving me hints. I've been seeing two of everything. Twin birch trees at the foot of our driveway. Twin beds in our hotel room last week when we had asked for a queen. I cracked an egg the other day that had two yolks in it. A cow on a neighboring farm had twin calves just yesterday. I could go on!"

"You don't have to," my mom said and pointed at the sky. There, floating in the middle distance, were two identical hot-air balloons as colorful as rainbows. My mom and I both gasped.

I was too young then to know that these "hints" from God are nothing to scoff at. I was amused at the time, but I've learned over the years to take these things very seriously. Call them hints, call them signs, or call them coincidences. They are God's way of communicating. Coupled with my "gut feeling" that I was carrying twins, there was ample evidence that the doctor and his theories were wrong.

Sure enough, when I lay down on the metal table and let the technician put her slimy wand on my belly, the evidence was clear. In fact, the technician nearly knocked me off the table with her belly laugh: "You were right, Mrs. Stokkermans!" she exclaimed in her thick Polish accent. "There are two babies! You see them right here... and here!" My mom and I laughed all the way back to the doctor's office, thrilled to tell him the news. It felt like God was there with us in the car, nudging me and smiling as if to say "I told you so!"

***

My twins—a girl and a boy—were born on November 2nd. The birth was hard work, but everything went smoothly and I felt great immediately afterwards. My only problem was an injection that I had received. It turned out I was allergic to it, and it made me very sick for a few days. Still, I was so happy to have my babies in my arms—one baby for each arm—and to have Frank by my side. What a beautiful family portrait we made from the very beginning! We named our babies Heather and Bradley, and as soon as I was able to get up and move around, I started "playing house" in real life. My vision of the perfect family had been realized. All that was missing was the picket fence, and Frank was handy enough to make that come true as well.

I thanked God with all my heart, but then my heart was young. In some ways, I was like a child who had been given just what she'd put on her Christmas list, and my gratitude was equal merely to the sum of those parts. It was too simple an equation. I had told God, "I want this," and he had given it to me. Saying "thank you" was easy; it required no effort from my soul. As I would learn all too soon, life does not always allow for such simple equations.

Nancy Stokkermans

8

Growing Up All of a Sudden

Life with twin babies was hard work, but it was just the kind of work I was cut out for. I won't pretend I made it look easy. There were days when I didn't get dressed at all, and if you looked under my couch cushions you might find any number of Cheerios or missing baby socks. But I loved the chaos of raising small children. In fact, I found a soothing rhythm in it. The day was organized by the needs and desires of these sweet, perfect creatures, and I could think of nothing more logical than following their lead. After all, were they not God's children, unstained and pure? Being with them reminded me of being with my wonderful niece, Cindy, but the love I felt for my own babies resonated on a different plane in my heart. They were the expressions of my soul, and my heart sang whenever I looked at their round little faces or wiped cereal off their fat little chins.

When the twins were one-and-a-half, I discovered I was pregnant again. Frank and I were both thrilled, as we had been planning to have a big family. The twins were gaining independence, and the house was ready to receive another little soul. So, we greeted the pregnancy with joy and enthusiasm.

When I was pregnant the first time, God gave me many hints about the fact that I was carrying twins. I had picked up on them, but didn't really take them seriously until I had the ultrasound to prove it. Even then, my main emotion was amusement. I had not yet learned to pay close attention to God's signs and signals, nor to heed the "gut feelings" and instincts that rose up from my own deepest being. These are important messages from God. He speaks in symbols and feelings, not words, but I had been too young and carefree to heed them.

With this pregnancy, similar phenomena occurred. I believe that while we are all recipients of God's messages, pregnant women are particularly susceptible. They are like lightning rods, poised to pick up on even the subtlest of signals. During my second pregnancy I noticed more signs than ever from God. This time, I was inclined to pay more attention to them, since they had been right during the previous pregnancy. The first and most significant sign was simply a feeling I had from day one of the pregnancy: a sense of heaviness, of an impossible weight. Yes, I was growing heavier as my body grew, but that wasn't it. It was a sense of unease, a sense of foreboding. I could never really put my finger on it or articulate it in words, but it was there all the time: a weight on my soul.

When I talked to Frank about it, he was upbeat. "Don't worry about it," he would say. "I'll bet lots of women worry during their second pregnancy. It's like you can't believe you could get lucky twice in a row, but you will. Everything will be fine." He would give my belly a little rub and kiss me on the forehead. I wanted to believe him.

Another of God's signs was even more tangible. Early in my second trimester, I started seeing apparitions. They looked like the spirits of children. They were ghostly in appearance, though not scary, and they floated ethereally at the thresholds of our rooms. I would see them drifting in and out of our bedrooms. They were the size of children, but they were featureless. The spirits did not seem particularly troubled, and they didn't seem to be trying to tell me anything. Nonetheless, they were there, plain as day, and they appeared several times each month.

I decided to tell Frank about them. I was worried that he'd think I was crazy, but I really wanted his calm, level-headed reassurance. What he told me shook me to the core.

"I see them too, Nancy."

"You... you mean..."

"Yes. I've been seeing them for a few months now. I thought it was just me. I've been trying to ignore them, but... it's impossible." Frank's eyes were wide. Gone was the reassuring gaze I was used to.

We didn't know what to make of this. Was there something in our drinking water that was making us both hallucinate? Were there some mischievous kids in the area playing tricks on us? The situation was eerie enough that we half hoped for an explanation like this, but the apparitions continued and came more frequently as the pregnancy progressed. Frank and I would sit in bed and watch, together, as the ghost of a small child entered the room and then left it just as quietly.

"Is it God trying to talk to us?" I asked.

"God? But what would He be telling us?" Frank wondered. He was used to the miracles in church, the ones he could understand, and the ones that were mediated by a priest.

"I don't know, Frank. Should we be scared?"

"I don't know. But I do know I don't *feel* scared," said Frank. "These ghosts, whoever they are, they don't seem threatening. They don't seem ominous. It's almost like they're friendly little visitors."

"How many of them do you think there are?" I asked.

"There could be hundreds, or there could just be one – the same one that we're seeing over and over again."

"That feels right to me. But who is this child? Is it the spirit of our unborn baby, coming to meet us in advance?" I giggled.

"Maybe it's the baby's way of sussing out the situation," Frank laughed. We both went to sleep with hopeful smiles on our faces, still unsure of what we were experiencing or why.

***

My pregnancy progressed, and we concentrated on preparing our twins for their new brother or sister. I fussed about, getting the house in order, while Frank worked hard on the farm, making sure there were no loose ends to tie up after the baby came. I woke up in the morning of September 14th, my due date, and realized that the dream I'd been having about ocean waves was actually a reaction to the waves of tension I was feeling in my abdomen. I was in labor. What a punctual baby, arriving right on schedule!

After a relatively easy labor—the second time is always easier than the first, they say—my beautiful baby was born. He was a strapping 8 pounds, 9 ounces, and he was magnificent. He looked just like an angel and smelled like heaven. His hair was light and matted to his soft head, and his lips were curled into a tiny smile. His feet were like little dumplings; I wanted to put them in my mouth. He was healthy and robust from the moment he was born, and he took to nursing like he'd been practicing for months. I inhaled his scent and gathered him in my arms, wiping off his delicious baby-slime with my own nightdress.

We named him Adam. I bonded with him instantly; there was no awkward period of adjustment. Frank, Heather, and Bradley bonded with him, too. I detected no sibling rivalry or jealousy, even though the twins were two years old and just discovering the concept of "mine." We were a family of five now, and I felt like the queen of a country. I couldn't believe my good fortune, and I thanked God for answering my prayers, for giving me another healthy baby.

I expected that once the baby was born, once I could see that he was healthy, the feeling of uneasiness would leave, and the apparitions would stop. I figured these things would disappear with the rest of my pregnancy symptoms, like swollen ankles and heartburn. The heavy feeling remained, however, and so did the apparitions. I was so caught up in caring for a newborn that I didn't have much time to dwell on these matters, but I wondered about them. I prayed almost nonstop to God to please keep my Adam safe. I loved him so much that my heart hurt. I did not think I could love anyone as much as I loved him.

***

Since Adam was born during harvest season, Frank was very busy and could not be with us very much although he squeezed in every minute he could to be with his newest baby. On one particular evening, Frank got home especially late. We ate a late dinner together because the children were all tucked safely into bed. At around 10:45 p.m., after Frank and I had gone to bed, Adam started to cry. This was unusual: Adam didn't tend to cry at this hour. I had nursed him and changed him, and that usually made him content, at least until the wee hours of the morning. Tonight was different, though, and his crying was insistent. Happy to give in, I entered his room and picked him up. He fussed a bit so I took him into our bedroom and sat on the bed beside Frank. The two of them played for a while, sharing silly smiles. After that, Adam seemed very content, so I put him back to bed. He went right to sleep without wanting to be nursed.

I awoke the next morning at 6:00 a.m. and wondered why Adam hadn't wakened to feed during the night. I was grateful for the extra sleep but confused about why he'd slept so long. I hurried to his room. I opened the door and peeked into his crib, and I knew. I knew without having to feel for his breath or his pulse, without having to try and shake him awake. My Adam was gone. My beloved baby, whose life had already overwhelmed me with a love unlike any I'd known, was dead.

I can't remember anything that happened after that moment. It was as if a flash bulb went off and temporarily blinded me. All the days and nights that followed were a blur of white pain as if the world was overexposed. I was paralyzed with grief. I had never known such joy as that which I'd felt in the days after Adam's birth, and now I was living in a world of pure pain. I was engulfed in grief, burning white hot, my core exploding. Life as I knew it had detonated.

People reached out to me, but all I remember from those early days are the desolate prayers I uttered to my God, the God who had forsaken me. *Why did You do this?* I pleaded with Him. *Why did You take my baby away? I was a good mother. All I did was love him unconditionally. I loved him so purely and so right. It was homage to You. Why did You punish me?* My tears were a flood. My breasts leaked milk.

I wanted God to take me, too, so I could see my Adam again. I wanted the chance to take care of him. Where was he, this tiny baby, all alone? He needed his mother. I needed to be with him. The need was an ache. There was no relief.

***

"You gain strength, courage and confidence by every experience in which you really stop to look fear in the face. You are able to say to yourself, "I lived through this horror. I can take the next thing that comes along." You must do the thing you think you cannot do.
—*Eleanor Roosevelt*

After a couple of weeks, I was able to emerge from the fog of grief and take a look at the debris field around me. Frank had been keeping the world spinning: the twins were clean, well-fed, and happy, and the house was in order. Everyone around us understood what we were going through, and no one balked at my grief. There were too many casseroles in our freezer to count, and people dropped in or called several times a day to check up on us. I had been well taken care of even if I'd been oblivious to it for days on end.

The doctor explained what had happened. Adam had died of SIDS, which stands for Sudden Infant Death Syndrome. It happens to about two percent of babies in North America, and no one knows exactly what causes it. Nowadays, doctors suggest that placing a baby to sleep on its back may help reduce the risk of SIDS and believe that certain factors like respiratory problems at birth can increase the risk. Although Adam always slept on his stomach, he never had a single problem with his breathing. It was just one of those things, my doctor said. He reassured us that it was nothing we did wrong: no negligence, no errors, no fault. Our baby had simply died, without reason, without warning.

As the reality of life without Adam began to sink in and I started to resume my normal rhythms with the twins, I was able to look at the situation more clearly. My anger at God subsided. I had been truly angry, I realized, though I had been in too much pain to lash out with more than a whimper. Now, as my heart started its long, arduous journey toward healing, I decided to ask God what all of this could mean.

In my conversations with God, most of which started with some variation on the theme of *Why me?*, I started having some interesting realizations. The first one was the most startling. I realized that the feeling of uneasiness and foreboding, the one that had tormented me throughout my pregnancy and through Adam's early days, had disappeared completely the moment I discovered he was gone. Of course, that feeling had been instantly replaced with grief, so you'll forgive me for not noticing right away. The foreboding was gone, and I felt nothing now but a strange calm. Although it was saturated with sadness, it was a peaceful calm. I thought back to the moment I found Adam in his crib, the moment the atomic bomb landed on my heart, and I realized that the awful feeling of doom had lifted then, like a wisp of vapour. Now, weeks later, I was free of it still.

"God," I asked, "is it your mercy that gives me this relief, even in my time of utmost pain?" For as grief-stricken as I felt without my Adam, I was so grateful to be released from that oppressive feeling of doom. It was like God had removed a thorn from my side, and I was finally able to feel the freedom from that pain.

Another amazing revelation I had was that the feeling of doom that God had been "torturing" me with throughout my pregnancy had actually been a gift. It was awful, yes, but it had made me pay close attention to every minute I spent with my precious baby. Because of this strange feeling, I had been sure to make every second count. I spent more time snuggling with him than I might have otherwise. I spent more time soaking up the sunshine of his smiles. I didn't let a single second pass without rejoicing in my baby and loving his life. So, when he died, I didn't feel as though I'd missed any chances. I had given everything I could to Adam, and I had received all his gifts to me. If it weren't for that feeling of foreboding, I might have been bereft of all these extra gifts.

Realizing that my sense of foreboding had been a direct warning from God, I knew it was time to start listening. Obviously, I could "hear" and interpret God's messages. It was a talent I was developing. For better or worse, I had this extra sense, and I vowed to hone my ability. One afternoon, I sat down in the rocking chair where I had nursed Adam and had a conversation with God.

"God, I've said a lot of angry things to You in the last few weeks. I've had nothing but pain inside me, and nothing but pain could come out. I'm healing, though, and I'm ready to remember joy."

I rocked in the chair, comforted by the familiar rhythm. I didn't have a baby in my arms, but I didn't feel alone either.

"I'm ready to say 'thank you,'" I said to God. "That's right: not 'why me' but 'thank you.' I thank you for the gift of your messages. If you hadn't sent me those warnings, I might not have been inspired to savour every moment with Adam, to seize the day every day he was here."

"I thank you for giving us that last snuggle with Adam on the night he died. If he hadn't fussed unexpectedly, we wouldn't have had that magical hour with him. I thank you, God, for giving me the talent of hearing and understanding your messages. I feel you have been talking to me all along, God, and I'm only now able to realize it. How many messages did I miss, in my youth? How many signs went unnoticed? I'm sorry for my naiveté, God. I'm wiser now, and I'm ready to learn your language."

As I sat in my chair that quiet afternoon, it was as though God was listening directly. I could feel His presence in the room. The curtains billowed softly as a breeze pushed at their hems. The creak of the rocking chair made a gentle, cozy song. Sunlight sprawled along the floorboards like a lazy cat. I felt calm, and I almost felt happy.

Suddenly, I remembered Adam's smile. It hit me like a gust of wind. His smile! His glorious, delirious smile! It was a smile no baby so young could possibly produce, yet he did, again and again. I sat in my chair, and I laughed out loud, remembering Adam's smile. His mouth, so small, would open up in an impossible grin, and his eyes would shine with mirth. His smile was all gums. Frank and I would get lost in that smile, overcome with joy. Adam's smile, that perfect event, God had given to us. Most babies don't smile until they are much older, but God gave Adam these early smiles so we could see them before he was gone.

"Thank you, God," I laughed, and I sat in my rocking chair, laughing and crying at the impossible miracle of Adam's little smile.

***

More weeks passed, and with each day I strove to face the sun again. It was hard at times, I still felt crippled by sadness, but I tried. I had faith that I would feel joy—if only an incomplete joy—again one day. My husband was loving and kind, and we helped each other recover. My twins, Heather and Bradley, were their usual, delightful selves, and they were reaching some of the more exciting milestones around that time: talking in full sentences, singing songs. I marvelled at their beauty, and sometimes I got down on the floor with them and just had *fun*.

I went to church every Sunday, like I had before Adam's death. People at church were kind to me though I got the impression that they were also uncomfortable. I understood. No one wants to get too close to the death of a child. However, I grew increasingly dissatisfied with my experiences at church. It was beginning to seem like people there were going through the motions—not just with me, but also with the service itself.

Perhaps it was because now, having experienced something so profound as the death of my child, I was able to see things as they were. Perhaps I had a different kind of vision. Now, when I looked around at the congregation, I saw them as nothing more than a group of well-dressed individuals, kneeling and standing, kneeling and standing, mouthing the words to the hymns. Where was the rapture? Where was the connection with God? Did these people feel differently when they left the church than they had felt when they went in? Were they touched by God? The answer seemed to be no. In that case, why was anybody even here?

I had to face the reality: the Catholic Church wasn't serving me very well, not during my time of particular need. I still loved the teachings, and I loved the priest's homilies. I loved singing the hymns and hearing the gospels. Yet, I felt like I was the only one there who did, and that made me feel lonely. Quite frankly, I felt closer to God when I was outside the church.

Lord, Did You Cry With Me When Mommy Hit Me?

Indeed, I talked to God nonstop. It was one of the things that got me through those difficult months. The prayer I uttered a thousand times a day was for God to take care of my Adam. I trusted that Adam was with God, but I wanted some reassurance that he was happy up there, safe in God's care. "Please God," I would pray, "give me some sign that my Adam is with You." I sent up this prayer more times than I could possibly count. I said it with nearly every breath.

Finally, one night, about six months after Adam's death, God answered my prayer. As I had learned to expect, the answer was not a literal response but a symbolic gesture. I was asleep in my bed, deep in the night. I woke with a start, jolted wide awake. I sat up in bed, not sure why I was doing it. Then, I gasped in amazement. There, beside my bed, was a being, an unnameable being, neither child nor adult, neither male nor female, wearing a robe of sparkling jewels. The being fluttered about three feet off the ground, radiating color and light. An incredible peace radiated from the being, and a beautiful look of sympathy came from its face. At that moment, I knew Adam was safe with God. The being disappeared from in front of me, and a feeling of peace filled the room and my heart. From that moment on, I knew I was going to make it. My son was safe. I never asked for confirmation again.

***

I had begun my marriage as an uncomplicated person with simple desires. I sent up a "wish list" to God and sat back, hoping to put checkmarks next to each item. I thought it was as simple as that, After all, they say "Ask and ye shall receive." However, it took a journey through the darkest depths of the ocean for me to realize the complexity of God's work, and I emerged with a mature understanding of my relationship with God. I had finally figured out how to communicate with Him in a meaningful way. I was finally gaining the ability to read and interpret his signs. I was finally "literate" in the language of God.

Now, my journey would take a new turn. It was time to use my knowledge and experience to find the path I belonged on, even if that meant blazing a brand-new trail.

9

Charting my own map

Most of the months and even years following Adam's death were spent doing little more than putting one foot in front of the other. Anyone who knows true grief knows this: for a long time, you are merely surviving. By putting one foot in front of the other, I was taking steps, and each step brought me closer to a place of peace. I would never forget my Adam—I still think of him every single day, without fail, and he died more than twenty-five years ago—but I felt myself coming back to life, little by little, day by day.

I found Sundays to be especially hard, though, even when I was feeling good during the week. It made sense: Sundays had always been hard for me. That was the day that my parents always fought the worst, the day the atmosphere in our house was at its most turbulent. I spent so many Sundays, as a child, watching my parents tear each other to emotional shreds, then watching my mother take her rage and sadness out on Kathy, then consoling my mother while she cried the day away. It was engrained in me from an early age to feel sad on Sundays. So, throughout my life, I found myself depressed on Sundays; it was a recurring theme. After Adam's death, it got worse, and at times I felt like I would never make it to Monday.

***

I got pregnant again soon after Adam's death. It was bittersweet. I still wanted to hold my baby Adam in my arms and wondered if I'd feel like I was "replacing" him with the new baby. At the same time, I was overjoyed. My heart was bursting with love, and I couldn't wait to share it with another little soul. In fact, an early ultrasound, coupled with my own intuition, revealed that I was pregnant with twins again. Two little souls! Two babies who could accept the outpouring of love from my aching heart!

I never had a moment of worry during the pregnancy. There were no premonitions, no apparitions; there was no fear at all. Gone was the sense of foreboding, and I enjoyed my pregnancy with confidence. I knew with utmost certainty that the birth would go well, and indeed it did. My second set of twins, another boy and another girl, were born easily and in perfect health. I revelled in their softness and gathered them in my arms, overflowing with gratitude.

We named the twins Holly and Gregory. Heather and Bradley were three and a half and jumped right into the roles of big sister and big brother. Frank and I laughed as we watched them interact with the newborn twins. On the one hand, it was lovely to see them try, while on the other hand it was nerve-wracking to see two clumsy toddlers meddling with their fragile little siblings. We often intervened.

Our life was sweet after the arrival of the twins, and we were thankful for what we had. Life, though, was also incredibly busy. I don't think you know what the word *busy* means until you've spent a day with four children under four. It took some adjusting to get used to it. Between the seemingly infinite diaper changes, the non-stop need for snacks, the round-the-clock breastfeeding, and the staggered naptime schedule, I often wished I could sprout an extra pair of arms. I envied the octopus. Not only that, but the children were at different developmental stages and had different personalities. Heather wanted me to run and climb with her; Bradley wanted me to build towers and assemble trains; and the twins both wanted to be held all the time. So, it felt impossible to keep them all happy. At times, I wondered if I was up to the task. I would look at the piles of laundry strewn around the house, sniff the air, wondering where that smell was coming from, see Frank's own exhaustion as he slumped home after a day of hard labor, and think, "What have we done to ourselves?"

I realized, though, over time, that every parent wonders that. We were doing our best. Our kids were healthy, and they were happy most of the time. That was enough. Once I grasped the concept that life isn't supposed to be neat and efficient all the time, I was able to sink my teeth into the role of motherhood and really fall in love with it. It dawned on me that I was a good Mom--What a concept!—and that my family was a happy one.

That said, I can't pretend that the pain of losing Adam wasn't a constant distractor. It was a huge one. I ached every day. It was like a thorn in the foot, something I felt with every single step. I worried sometimes that it would unravel me. Some days, I would be playing happily with the twins, oblivious to my own simmering pain, when suddenly it would erupt as if from nowhere. I would find myself sobbing uncontrollably and would have to run to the bathroom to compose myself lest I upset the children. I found myself breaking down in public as well, completely without warning. If I saw a baby at the grocery store who reminded me of Adam, I would be a mess in an instant, running to my car to hide. I broke down once in church, to the sympathetic stares of the other parishioners.

I knew I was still grieving Adam, but the intensity of my grief, as well as my inability to control when and where it expressed itself, started to worry me. I wondered if I were going crazy. If I were crazy, would I turn out like my mother? What if it were an inevitable fate? What if Adam's death just happened to be the event that precipitated it? Turning into my mother was one of my worst fears, and the loss of control I felt around my own grief was scaring me. I prayed to God to hold onto me, to hold tight so I wouldn't fall apart. I sought comfort at church but still felt a vague emptiness when I was there. I needed some concrete help—fast. I started to see a psychiatrist.

During my sessions with the doctor, I felt free to let my sadness out. I poured it out in a great flood, all over the poor man! I held nothing back. It was extremely liberating to be able to talk about my grief with someone who didn't also share it. During the course of my treatment, I also described my new fear of losing another child. It was growing every day and becoming irrational. I was afraid to let any of my children out of my sight. I had terrible, involuntary daydreams about bad things happening to them, and when I had these, it felt like I was having a heart attack. I also told the doctor about my lifelong fear of becoming like my mother.

He was a gentle man, an unflappable listener. I tried to imagine just how much sadness, grief, and anxiety had been dumped all over his desk over the years. How many sad stories had he heard? How many slumped shoulders had he patted? How many boxes of tissue had been used up in this office? He was good at his job: he allowed me to empty myself out and then build myself up again. He explained that everything I was feeling, even the stuff that felt crazy, was perfectly sane. He made me feel normal, even healthy. He made me feel like my grief was *right*, like I was a sane person responding sanely to an awful event. He explained the seven stages of grief and helped me understand how my feelings fit into that model. He made me sure I would be okay someday, and he made me realize I needed patience. He made me forgive myself, and trust myself, and give myself permission to grieve.

I finished my sessions with the doctor feeling empowered. No, I was not "cured," but I knew that I didn't need to be. I began to think of the therapy sessions in the context of church and in the context of prayers and conversations with God. Were my sessions with the doctor a little bit like my conversations with God? Well, yes. They were mostly one-sided since it is a proper therapist's job to sit back and listen, to let *you* do the talking, and they involved the quiet, gentle presence of the doctor, a wise man who wanted the best for me and held the promise of my recovery. I laughed to think of my doctor wearing a nametag that said "God." He was too humble for any such notion! I figured, though, there was something to the idea that I could compare the experience of therapy with the experience of prayer.

This got me thinking: what else? Were there other analogies I could draw? Perhaps going to church had a similar effect: it allowed me to focus my thoughts, just like going to the psychiatrist's office allowed me to focus. In both settings, I could spend a full hour dedicated to the task of examining my psyche, my fears, my hopes, and my relationship with God.

Church, prayer, therapy: three disparate things with some significant elements in common. It was dawning on me: there is more than one path leading to God. There is no right way, no wrong way. There are many ways, and as long as you are moving forward, you will get there.

***

After my realization that I might be able to create my own map showing the way to God, *my* way to God, I started doing lots of reading. I read books on spirituality and religion as well as books on personal healing. I wanted to find out everything I could, not just about what other people understood about God but also about what was going on inside myself. I became an addict, spending lots of time at the library and the bookstore, feasting on the information I found there. I added "books" to my list of things that would lead me to God and made them part of my map.

I continued going to church every Sunday with Frank and the kids, but I was growing increasingly restless. I loved the service and had nothing in particular against the Catholic Church, but it wasn't enough. I wanted the church, but I wanted more as well. I had my books, my diverse self-education about world religions and spirituality, and my own soul-searching, but still I felt I needed something more. I prayed to God to help me figure out what it was, to help me find it. In a way I felt that this sense of yearning was in itself a sign from God: He wanted me to find my way to Him, and this was how He was helping me do it. I prayed for more guidance. I promised to be on the lookout for His signs.

***

One afternoon, just after I had taken the babies out of the bath, a gentleman came to my door. I was up to my elbows in talcum powder and normally would have called for the visitor to come back later, but something compelled me to answer the door. The man introduced himself as Steve and said he was from the Gospel Hall. He asked if he could talk with me. I instantly felt good about him, so I invited him in. He overlooked the mess and didn't mind the twins scrambling all over me, half-dressed. After one conversation with Steve, I knew it was God who had sent him to me. In fact, I asked Steve why he had stopped at my home, and he told me that he had been driving by and had received a message to pull into my driveway. "Something just told me that someone here needed my help," he said. I gasped. God had clearly intervened. Immediately, a great friendship began between Steve and me.

Steve came to my home periodically and talked with Frank and me about God. Frank, who was happy in the Catholic Church and loyal to his family's traditions, wanted nothing to do with the message Steve brought us. Usually, Frank would leave us alone, and Steve and I would explore God together. Frank trusted me and wasn't jealous of the friendship I was developing, but at the same time he wasn't happy with the idea of my leaving the Catholic Church. I tried to explain to him that I'd felt unsatisfied at church and that my acceptance of Steve's ideas didn't mean I was renouncing Catholicism; in fact, I was only augmenting it. But Frank was firm: he wanted me to keep attending our church, mostly because he wanted our children to continue in the Catholic faith. I could understand his devotion to this tradition although I was frustrated with his skepticism. So, to keep everyone happy, I went to The Gospel Hall during the week and to our Catholic church on Sundays.

During Steve's visits to our home, he explained his own beliefs as well as the basic tenets of the Gospel Hall. He told me that in order to be allowed into the Kingdom of God, one had to be born again. The idea was intriguing to me, but intimidating. On the one hand, I loved the idea of starting over, of meeting Jesus as if for the first time and accepting Him with the innocence of a newborn child. On the other hand, how would I ever accomplish the emotional rigor necessary to be born again? At times, I felt like a complete mess. How would I make myself worthy of being saved? I asked Steve a million questions, and I prayed to God to guide me in the right direction. Was the Gospel Hall part of my journey? I paid attention to Steve's teaching and listened hard for messages from God.

The premise of the Gospel Hall's message seemed simple: in order to be saved, I had to accept that Jesus had died for my sins. I had to accept that He had, very literally, stood in as my proxy on that day, suffering on my behalf, serving my sentence for me. Indeed, all of humanity has a huge debt of sin, for we are all sinners, and Jesus selflessly offered to endure our punishment for us in exchange for our salvation. What an incredible gift! It was almost impossible to wrap my head around that kind of selflessness, though I felt grateful without even having to think about it. So, that part was easy: accept that Jesus died on the cross so that we might have a chance to enter heaven. Done.

But the rest was more complicated. I had to accept that glorious fact, but then I had to agree to be born again myself: to be baptized, to begin anew, and to announce my faith in the Gospel Hall. This would be harder. Look at what I was up against. First, there was Frank and his steadfast family who were immovably loyal to the Catholic Church. Then, there was my entire community of neighbors, friends, and fellow parishioners who could never imagine leaving the Catholic Church. I risked judgment, scorn, and disappointment from all of these people. What's more, I knew that even if I managed to be saved, my family was still at risk. They would have to follow me. I would have to convince them. After all, what good would it be to make it to heaven only to discover that my husband and children were consigned to stay out? It was a lonely prospect. So, how on earth would I persuade them to follow my lead? The task seemed utterly daunting.

Nevertheless, I knew I wanted it. I had been best friends with Jesus since the days when my mother read Bible stories to us as children. I knew God intimately, and there was nothing I wouldn't do for Him. So, I resolved to allow myself to be born again and to lead by example. I could only hope that my family would follow me.

10
Seeing the Whole Picture

Frank wouldn't come with me to the Gospel Hall, but he was magnanimous enough not to give me a hard time about it. He let me go with his blessing. On one occasion, after I had tiptoed through the doors, a little nervous about being there alone, I noticed that my friend Steve was the guest speaker for the evening. I listened to him speak, and though I had spent countless hours listening to him in the context of my own living room, there was something different about tonight. I knew that evening when I was truly saved, when the spirit of Jesus truly entered me. I watched Steve speak as if he were an angel hovering before me. His words, while they were words I'd heard before, suddenly came to life.

I felt it in the deepest part of my bones. I felt it in my blood. I was human, beloved by God. I was a regular human who tried hard and sometimes failed. I was someone who strove to be good but who sinned nonetheless. And Jesus loved me. Jesus loved me! He loved me *even though* I sinned; He loved me more than I could ever realize. He loved me like I loved my children, like I loved my baby Adam; His love for me was infinite. I was totally unworthy of His love *yet He loved me*. He loved me enough to die for me. Jesus loved me that much.

The realization nearly knocked me out of my seat. Jesus loved me, and that was what made me worthy. *I was worthy of Jesus's love simply because He loved me.*

I wept. Tears rolled down my cheeks and onto my collar. I felt my chest heaving. I cried openly right there amid a room full of strangers. I didn't care, and nobody stared. They expected this. They had probably been there themselves. I wept with joy, with rapture. I felt my soul soar.

For someone who grew up in a house with parents who couldn't love me as I tried to be perfect, it was remarkable to realize that Jesus could love me even with all of my flaws. This was the definition of unconditional love. I was feeling it right now, and it was enough to knock me to the floor. I made eye contact with Steve. From his position at the front of the hall, he had seen me break down into joyful, transformative tears, and he knew what was going on. He smiled warmly. His eyes shone.

***

After my experience at the Gospel Hall, I knew I was on the right path. I talked to Frank and the children about it. While they were happy for me, they didn't fully understand, but I was convinced and talked to God about it at every opportunity.

"God," I said, one morning alone in my living room. "I know now what it feels like to recognize and bask in your love. I don't just want to 'talk the talk' about Jesus, I want to 'walk the talk.' But it's hard, Lord. Leaving the Catholic Church is hard; blazing a new trail is hard." I looked out the window at the hydrangeas blooming in my front garden like tufts of whipped cream. Their beauty was intoxicating, another sign of God's love.

"I will look for signs from You. I want to know what to do next. I want to lead by example, Lord, and I want my family to follow me. Give me a sign about how to proceed, and I will take up the task with joy," I said. I expected to wait a few days, a few weeks. I expected to be on the lookout for subtle signals from God, but on this day, He chose to speak to me directly. It was the first time this had ever happened, and it was as if lightning struck.

In a voice that was not mine but that didn't seem to come from anywhere, there came the words, "Go under. Go under the water." I fell to my knees.

"Go under the water. Submerge." I listened carefully to this voice, this non-voice, this strange echo. Was it loud? Was it silent? I couldn't say.

"Submerge," it said once more, and in an instant I knew what it meant. God was speaking to me, and He was telling me to be baptized in the Gospel Hall. It was clear.

"I will do as you ask, Lord," I said and wept with gratitude.

***

Behind the altar at the Gospel Hall sits a large tub. The tub is filled with water, and each person being baptized is completely submerged by one of the elders of the community. I stood at the altar on my baptism day and knew that what I was doing was right. I had followed God's road signs, and they had led me here. I had never felt so sure of anything in my life.

The elders of the Gospel Hall had encouraged me to invite as many people as I wanted as guests at my baptism. I did even though I was nervous about what my friends and family would think. I knew many of them would find the event strange, but I wanted them to have what I had—the chance to be saved. I also wanted to honor the Lord by showing Him I was not afraid to follow His wishes.

As I let my body fall into the hands of the elders, I surrendered to God at the same time. They submerged me in the water, and I felt it surround me. It was neither cool nor hot; it was the temperature of my own body. I felt total peace, and I let my limbs float in the undulating water. It covered my face; it entered my ears; it enveloped me. I was calmly joyful. I was giving a gift to God and receiving one from Him in the process.

***

My baptism was a very big step in my spiritual journey. I was grateful to have received such clear guidance from God and confident that I was on the right path. I felt proud to know that I could hear His messages and happy to honor them, but I was also confused. While I was glad that God had wanted me to be baptized and born again, I wondered why He did not request this of all his children. Why me and not Frank? Why me and not my children, or my sister Kathy, or any of my beloved friends? It was a paradox. This was an occasion of great honor but also a time of anguish. How would I guarantee the salvation of my loved ones?

As it turns out, I needed only to trust in God. Decades later, it is clear to me that God will call His children, each in his or her turn. My time came in that difficult year after the death of my baby. That was when God felt it was right for me. The time for other members of my family and community would be different. Two of my children have already been saved, and they came to it in their own time. My oldest daughter, Heather, struggled with being saved for many years. She wanted it very badly but found herself on an arduous path. Finally, while praying in the Catholic Church during her second year at the university, Heather felt Jesus enter her and knew she was saved. I had struggled for years to teach her the value of accepting Jesus and tried to force her into the position I was in. As it turns out, Heather needed to be saved in her own time, when she was ready. Once she was ready, it was easy. For Heather, a mix of the teachings from the Catholic Church, from the Gospel Hall, and from her own reading and reflections led her to God.

My youngest son, Gregory, was saved during a Gospel meeting at the age of seven. How fortunate for him to find God at such a young age! I had worked hard for many months to be saved, and my seven-year-old son had nailed it so quickly. This was further proof for me that there is no "right" path toward God and that each person must find his or her own path. My path had been different from Heather's, whose path had been different from Gregory's. My other children, and their children, are on paths of their own. Whether they are saved tomorrow or twenty years from now, I know it will happen when it should. It is not for me to say, and it is not for me to worry. All I need to do is lead by example, and that's what I've done. I found my path; I cleared the brambles away; and I am following it steadfastly to this day.

***

My understanding of this path analogy—that every person must find her own path before she can even begin to follow it and that no two people will be on the same path—has been honed over decades of experience. I look back to my earliest days with God, when I was a frightened child hunched over her bedside, praying frantically. How I hoped that God would befriend me and listen to my prayers! In those early days, I sought God with the heart of a child: innocent but naïve. I was unaware that there was more to praying than merely asking for what you want, and I wasn't mature enough to see that God was communicating with me in ways that weren't obvious, weren't literal.

I look back to the era after Kathy's pregnancy when I began to realize that God's relationship with me was more complex than I had thought. I saw that the same God who could allow such pain in Kathy's life could also give her the one thing that brought her perfect joy: her daughter Cindy. I saw that joy could come from pain and that pain could come from joy. I saw that prayers could be answered in roundabout ways. I learned to look for God's messages with a more discerning eye.

I look back to the era in my early marriage when I was happy but knew something was missing. This was the beginning of my search for my own true path. I had everything I wanted but felt that there was more I could do to get closer to God, and I learned that to be truly close to God I would have to work hard to grow up.

I look back to the era after Adam's death when I learned that there is nothing simple or easy about a life with God. I learned about the infinitely intricate nuances of love. I learned that joy and pain can co-exist, that hope can spring from despair, and that love can transcend even death.

I look back to the era when I left the Catholic Church and entered the Gospel Hall and felt the strange twinges of fear and excitement about cutting my own path. Those were the early days of trail-blazing, and to me it felt dangerous and exhilarating, like I was an explorer, forging a path through the frontier of a new continent.

Then, there is now, when I look back only a day or two to where I'm at today. I am a grandmother, blessed with eight beautiful grandchildren who fill my heart with love and my belly with laughter. I am a mother, proud to have raised my four incredible children and to have preserved the sacred memory of my Adam. I am a friend to so many wonderful men and women that I sometimes feel as rich as a queen. I am my own best friend, as well, now that I'm on my own. After thirty-three years of marriage, Frank and I decided to go our separate ways though we love each other and hold each other in high esteem. After we sold our business and said goodbye to our children and they left the nest, we realized there was very little left of "us." What's more, Frank's vision of God's kingdom was very different from mine, and our respective paths seemed to be tripping each other up. We separated amicably and are still on good terms, still proud of the family we raised together and the life we built.

I am also a child of God, still searching. I am confident about the path I've found, but I am always looking and listening for signs from God about where to go next. This is a journey; it doesn't end. There is no point at which you get to say, "There, I've made it. I can put down my pack and call it a day." No. It is indeed the pursuit of your path that keeps you filled with joy and close to God. I am still learning every day and still asking God for help. Day in and day out, as I take my surefooted steps on my path, I learn. I am open. I await instructions. I listen closely.

I have become adept at hearing God's messages, at reading the signs in God's language. I have dedicated my life to the task, and I have a bit of knowledge to share. I don't presume to have all the answers—or even most of them! I know that my path is mine alone and that each of us must find our own way, but I want to share my understanding—and God wants me to share it, too. This book is my means of doing just that. In the final chapter, I will outline some of the simple tools in my toolbox of life that have got me to where I am: safely and firmly planted on my path, heading in the right direction.

Nancy Stokkermans

11
What Worked for Me

Everybody is different. Everyone's life is different, everyone's experience of God is different. Even everyone's experience of reading this book is different. There is no way I could sit here with a straight face and try to tell you how to live your life with God. There is no prescription; there is no single set of rules. This is not a how-to book.

But we are a social species, and we learn from one another. So, I am here merely to offer you stories about what has worked for *me*. You can adapt the ideas so that they work for you in the context of your life and within the framework of your beliefs. You can translate the terms into your own personal "language." When I say God, you can think a higher power, mother nature, the universe, Allah, or whatever suits you best. When I say "pray," you can think "talk to the cosmos" or "engage in deep self-reflection." When I talk about angels, you can think about the things on earth that remind you of the heavens.

So, in my final chapter, now that my story has been told, I will tell you about a few of the tools and measures that have led me, speaking for myself alone, to where I am. They worked for me, and they continue to work as I continue to work hard in my quest for spiritual fulfillment. This has been *my* recipe; please see how it suits your own spiritual appetite.

Tool #1: Trust your instincts.

This is probably the first and most important thing I learned on my journey toward God. Your instincts or intuitions—those gut feelings you might recognize once in a while—are direct messages from God. It took me many years to realize it, but it made sense once I did. These feelings, so profound and unavoidable, seemed to be coming from the deepest part of my being. That's where God resides, isn't it? That's how He gets through to you if you let Him.

I've already told you the story about my instincts during my pregnancy with Adam. I *knew* something was going to happen, and I acted on that intuition by loving my baby with more passion and attention than I ever would have otherwise. When he was taken from me, I realized my instinct had been bang-on, and I was deeply grateful for it.

Now, let me tell you another story about a time my instincts guided me because I allowed them to. My youngest son, Greg, was about thirteen years old. He had been invited to his friend Mike's house to play. Greg had been to Mike's house many times. They were good friends, and I trusted Mike's parents. However, on this particular day, I was struck with a terribly uneasy feeling. It was pure dread. I could barely swallow it, but I kept it to myself as I drove Greg to Mike's house since Greg was so keen to go. I wrestled with myself: was I simply being paranoid? Had Adam's death affected me so that I was now irrationally overprotective of my other kids? I didn't know what to do. I wanted to be a "fun" Mom, but this feeling of dread was nearly overwhelming.

I dropped Greg off and, against my better judgment, drove home. The feeling of dread only increased. I went inside and timidly entered Greg's bedroom. That's when I felt it. Death. The room was dark even though it was the middle of the afternoon, and the air felt still and cold. All I could feel was death. I knew what death felt like. I had experienced it with Adam.

I gasped and began crying. "I get it," I said to God. "I'm sorry it took me so long to listen." I ran down the stairs two at a time, grabbed my keys, and leaped into the car. It was a forty-five minute drive to Mike's house, and I feared for my son the whole time. When I finally arrived, I pulled up the long driveway and saw Greg standing on the front step with his overnight bag in his hand. I cried tears of gratitude and relief.

"Why were you waiting on the porch?" I asked him.

"I knew you were coming," he said. When I pressed him for details, he didn't offer many, and I thought about what a sensitive boy I had. As we talked, however, Greg revealed that Mike's plans for the rest of the afternoon had included a rather dubious adventure: jumping from snow bank to snow bank on the frozen lake behind his house.

It was late February. The ice on the lake was thin and slushy. The lake was deep. Mike's parents were busy inside the house. I imagined what might have happened had Greg stayed. I thanked God, silently and then out loud, for making my instincts speak to me so loudly. My son, Greg, thanked me for heeding them.

Tool #2: Trust your children.

I have talked about how small children are as close to God as any human can be and that we are lucky to be in their company when we can be. When I was a child myself, I beheld the miracle that was my little niece Cindy, and I knew even then that I was in the presence of a sacred being. Children are pure, and if we take care not to stifle or disrupt their connection to God, we may be allowed to bask in it.

My own daughters, Heather and Holly, are my inspiration on this matter. They have five children between them, and as I watch the way they mother them, I realize they understand more about the sacredness of children than anyone else I know.

Heather and Holly trusted their children from the moment they were born, and they allow the babies to guide them. When their newborn babies cry, they feed them even if their doctor or nurse has told them to wait. If they cry in the night they hold them close even if their friends and peers have told them to train the babies to sleep through the night. If their toddler wants to snuggle, they indulge him even if their community encourages independence, and if their school-age child says he is too sick to go to class, they believe him, even if there is an important lesson that day. Are their children spoiled? Are they overly coddled? On the contrary. They are five of the most self-assured, sensitive, level-headed, and *happy* children I've ever seen.

Think about it: most people, when they have a baby, take her home from the hospital and follow all the rules they've been given. New mothers and fathers do this because they are nervous and unsure: they've never done this before! So, they can be forgiven. However, when these "rules" and standards include medical advice such as "keep your baby on a sleep schedule" or "feed your baby only every three hours and never at night" or when they include such social advice as "let Great-aunt Marge hold the baby to show respect" or "put the baby in her finest clothes when Grandpa Tucker is visiting," we stray too far from nurturing the natural instincts of the child. What does a baby want? To be held by her mother, to be fed when hungry. These are simple, sacred needs, and we do a disservice to our children, to ourselves, to the future of our own communities, and to God when we decide to ignore these simple instincts.

Tool #3: Trust angels, and let them help you.

All my life, growing up, I knew there was somebody watching out for me. I didn't know who it was, and I didn't really care. I just I sensed a presence and was grateful. I have talked at some length about angels on earth—people and animals that have been sent by God to soothe, assist, or save us. The existence of these angels on earth is evidence enough for me that we are surrounded by angels all the time. For this reason, I have found it helpful to have visual reminders, physical "proof" of the presence of angels on earth. I keep statuettes of angels all around my house and in my car. I even carry one in my purse. There is nothing particularly special about the angels I have. Some are made of clay, some of glass, and some of plastic. Some are as big as dolls; some are as tiny as thimbles. The figurines themselves are not sacred, but they represent the sacred that is all around us. They serve as reminders that the world is actually a sacred place.

Angels are charged with the special duty of protecting us. It took me some time to get used to the idea that I am allowed to ask for their help, but now I feel comfortable doing it. The *Bible* has a passage (*Revelation* 22:8-9) in which John prepares to fall down and worship at the feet of an angel, but the angel stops him. "I am a fellow servant," the angel tells him. He is given permission to accept help from the humble angel. I have taken this to heart. Don't laugh, but I've even talked to my angels to help me find a parking space! If I have my grandchildren with me in the car and the weather is inclement, I politely ask my angels to get us in the door safely. So far, they have always obliged.

Be sure to thank the angels when you pray to them. They are your kind friends, and they deserve your courtesy as well as your blessings. I feel close to my angels the way I feel close to my lifelong friends: ours is an easygoing relationship. It works!

My angel ever at my side, how lovely you must be --
To leave your home in Heaven, to guard someone like me."
My Guardian Angel

Tool #4: Pray even when you don't have to.

Many of us pray when times are tough: your marriage is shaky, your friend is sick, your job is unsatisfying. You get down on your knees. What about the times when everything is going along smoothly or when things can actually be classified as *great*? Not many people remember to pray during these times. It seems like simple advice, but it's something I've forgotten to do on too many occasions. Nowadays, I never forget. I pray just to check in. I pray just to say thank you. I pray, and I don't ask for anything at all. In this way, I stay connected to my God, and I remain mindful of the good things in my life.

Tool #5: Love your enemies—or at least, like them.

This is an oldie but a goodie, isn't it? I can't speak highly enough about the wonders this practice has done for me. In everyone's life, including mine, there are a handful of people we just don't get along with. Our personalities don't mesh, or perhaps we're downright antagonistic. It happens! In my past, I would think nasty thoughts about people like this and even indulge in negative gossip about them. No more. I have found it to be infinitely more satisfying to *bless* these people instead.

On more than one occasion, I have found myself thinking an unfriendly thought about someone I don't particularly like, and the next thing I know, I've stubbed my toe or been stung by a bee. It has happened too many times to be a coincidence: I think something mean, and then I get hurt. Not seriously hurt, but it's enough to get my attention. As a result of these little not-so-subtle hints from God, I've taken to thinking kindly thoughts about my enemies and antagonists. The guy who took my precious parking spot? I hope he finds exactly what he's looking for in the supermarket. The doctor who tried to brush off my questions? I hope the rest of her day is peaceful, calm, and gratifying. The teenager who blew a smoke ring in my face? I hope his iPod battery lasts forever. I don't know about you, but I find it vastly more comforting to wish happiness, love, and light on the people in my life who bother me than to waste my time or breath on complaining.

Tool #6: Use mantras and affirmations.

A mantra is a word or phrase that takes on greater spiritual or emotional significance as it is repeated and absorbed into the psyche. I have several mantras that I use in different situations, depending on what I need to focus on. If I'm stressed out in my life, I will repeat the word "calm" over and over until it is embedded in my mind. I will visualize the written word; I may even write it down. If I am having trouble in a relationship, I will use "peace" as my mantra. If I am feeling dark and depressed, I will use the word "light." The list goes on. I cannot overstate the power of the written or spoken word in my life: words have saved me, time and time again. (Perhaps that's why I decided to write a book!)

Similar to mantras are affirmations, phrases or sentiments that can be repeated to help you achieve psychic wellness. Some of my favorites are "Think twice and then think again" (I use this when I'm having trouble with financial impulse control), "I will be consistent in thought and action" (I use this when I want to practice what I preach), and "Happiness comes from within" (I use this one every day). Repeating and thinking something over and over can make it true. Again, this speaks to the power of the word. I believe so firmly in this that I put sticky notes around my house when I'm trying to make a change for the positive. I'll walk past the hall closet and see "I openly and willingly receive from others" emblazoned on the door. I'll look in the bathroom mirror and see "I will not judge others or myself" stuck to the glass. I have these colorful little squares all over the place: "I have a beautiful heart;" "I have miles to go before I reach my destination;" "I am a serene and tranquil person;" "I seek new solutions to old problems." In my experience, if I invoke these simple words in my head, out loud, or on paper, I can make them become my reality.

Tool #7: Make a vision board.

I learned this one from my friend and advisor Sue Maes. At first glance, it seems too good to be true, but I've used it, and it works. To make a "vision board," simply take a large piece of Bristol board (you can get one at any craft or dollar store) and give it a title. Its title will be your foremost wish. For example, if you're looking for someone to spend the rest of your life with, its title will be "My Ideal Mate." If you're looking for a job you can truly feel satisfied in, its title will be "My Ideal Job."

Draw a circle in the middle of the board and write the title inside it. In the top right corner, write your name, the date, and the time-frame in which you're hoping to achieve your goal. Next, draw lines radiating out from the center, and at the end of each line, write a word that describes the thing you're wishing for. For example, if you're looking for your ideal mate, write the qualities you're looking for in that person. Let your imagination roam: write down as many words as you feel you need. Finally, place your picture in the center of the circle and enjoy.

But beware: the vision board relies on words, so you have to choose your words carefully. Don't be vague. Don't write that you're looking for someone "nice." Be specific: you're looking for someone who is kind to animals, is generous with affection, or laughs often. As well, be careful not to use negative words. This means that instead of writing down attributes that you *don't* want, write down the ones you *do* want. If you write that you're looking for a job that isn't boring or that involves no long commute, you may just get the opposite of what you want. The universe doesn't recognize "isn't," "doesn't," or "won't." Focus on the positive: write that you want a job that is creative and stimulating and that is conveniently located or in-home. Finally, try to avoid using too many adjectives that focus on the physical, especially if you're describing a person. If your board is full of requests for someone who is handsome, strong-jawed, or tall, you're skewing the overall impression away from what matters. Concentrate on the person you want to *know*, not the person you want to *see*.

When you've finished creating your vision board, stick that thing under your bed or inside a closet, and forget about it. When you wake up in the morning, send a prayer up to God or the universe: *God, please help me find my ideal mate* (or job, or friend, or house), in the evening just as you are preparing to go to bed remember to thank God for sending you your ideal mate. Then, go to sleep, putting it out of your mind. Let the universe take care of it from there.

Sounds simple, right? It sounded too simple to me, too, until it worked more effectively than I ever could have hoped. Let me tell you two quick stories about my experience with vision boards. The first one was a learning experience; the second was my reward.

After the breakup of my marriage with Frank, I was ready for a new beginning. I wanted to share my life with someone, and I wanted God's guidance in finding that person. I made a vision board with—you guessed it—"My Soul Mate" as its title. I wrote down everything I wanted in a mate, and I let the universe do its thing. To my great surprise, I met the very person I had described on my board a few months later. He fit almost all the criteria I had written on the board, as far as I could tell, and I was blown away by how well it had worked. I embarked on an exciting relationship with this man, thinking I was on the right path. Well, that path took a turn, and things got dark. I found out, in time, that this man was not the person I had asked God to help me find. On the contrary, there were certain things about him that were precisely what I had been trying to avoid! Those were the things that caused our unpleasant breakup. Sad and confused, I pulled out my old vision board to see if I could figure out what went wrong.

There it was, plain as day: on the board, I had written (in big, bold letters, near the top) that I wanted someone who was not possessive, who was not jealous, and who was not aggressive. Well, I learned my lesson right there and then. This man was all of those things, in spades. They were three of the most important criteria for me, but since I had written the word "not" in each example, the universe simply gave me what it thought I wanted: a possessive, jealous, aggressive man. I was wiser for this lesson, let me tell you!

When I was ready to try again, I redid my vision board. This time, I chose my words meticulously. No negatives, nothing vague, nothing that could be misconstrued. I wrote down sixty words. I put the board under my bed and my faith in God. Please remember to write 90 days at the top of your board and the date that you are preparing it. On my second vision board, I wrote in the center "My Ideal Mate" instead of soul mate as I have since learned there is a great deal of difference in the two choices.

It was only a few months later that I met Ross. This story has a happy ending. Ross is everything I had hoped for—well, fifty-nine out of the sixty things I had hoped for, anyway! We are happy and secure together, and we complement each other perfectly. My kids and grandkids love him, and he is deeply devoted to family. Ross is an incredible person, and I can't wait to spend the rest of my life loving him. I know that he is meant to be with me on my path, and I thank God for helping me find him. He truly is my ideal mate who has a heart that is bursting with love, kindness and spiritual love for anyone at any time.

Did the vision board help me find Ross? I can't say for sure, but it seems like more than a coincidence to me. How does a vision board work? Again, I don't know, but it's possible that the simple act of writing down everything you want and taking care to curate those desires so that they are valid and make sense play a big role in helping you search effectively. It's possible that writing down all those words and sticking them under your bed, i.e. relegating them to your unconscious where you can do the work of searching without letting your fickle intellect get in the way play a role as well. Whatever is happening—call it self-help, divine intervention, whatever you will—all I can tell you is that it works.

Tool #8: Look for signs in unlikely places.

This is not just a piece of advice; it is the crux of this book and the principle by which I live my whole life. If there is one thing I've learned over the years, it's that God is always communicating with us but that we are not always able to discern His messages.

Imagine you are a tourist. You find yourself in a small train station in rural Italy, and you've left your phrasebook on the train. You're looking for a place to stay. You glance around frantically, staring at sign after sign after sign, looking for the word *hotel*. You don't see it anywhere. You feel homeless, lost, bereft. If only you knew that the Italian word for *hotel* is *pensione*, you would see that this very word is emblazoned on dozens of signs all around you. You aren't homeless at all; you're well taken care of. There is food, shelter, and a cozy fireplace waiting for you right around the corner if you could only see the signs in front of your face.

This is what it can be like to live a life oblivious to the messages of God. I lived this way for most of my young childhood, suffering, praying, and pleading to God. I expected that He would answer me directly by giving me the things I wanted, like giftwrapped boxes. It was only after I learned to look for His messages in unlikely places that I realized He'd been answering me all along.

To this day, I continue to be surprised by the ways God communicates with me. I have told you already about intuition and gut feelings. These are some of the most direct messages God sends, but there are other, more subtle ones. You might even call them playful. For example, I find that God gets my attention through music. If I am struggling with a dilemma in my life, I might ask God for guidance and receive it in the form of a radio song! One evening, after a particularly bad day, I was soaking in my bathtub, hoping to wash away my sorrows. I may have been wallowing; there may have been some self-pity. I asked God to help me get through this feeling, and just then I heard a song wafting in from the radio in the next room: "Rose Garden" by Lynn Anderson. The lyrics talk about how we can't always have what we want and that sorrow is just as valuable as joy. After all, the roses need rain so they can grow.

On another occasion, I was involved in a particularly frustrating argument with a store clerk. He wouldn't see my side of the story no matter how clearly I explained it, and my anger was mounting. Just then, the store speakers played a Muzak version of Donovan's "May as Well Try and Catch the Wind." In an instant, I took the message to heart and gave up my pointless quest. I wasn't going to win any argument with this guy even if I was right. It was as useless as trying to catch the wind. I left the clerk to his blustering. I thanked God for giving me perspective just when I needed it.

God speaks to me through music all the time, but everyone has their own way of talking to God. Maybe you will start to notice that newspaper headlines are particularly relevant to questions you've been asking God. Maybe you'll overhear snippets of other people's conversations and feel a frisson: it's as if they were talking directly to you! Maybe it will be a crossword puzzle, a poem, or something as profane as a TV commercial. It doesn't matter. If it speaks to you, listen. It could be a message from God in translation.

***

Like I said, I don't presume to know exactly how to live life in communion with God. I only know how to live *my* life that way, and I only came to this understanding after years of arduous effort and many mistakes. I learned. I struggled. I triumphed. I kept going. I have been through a lot of hardship—more than some, less than others—and I have survived it. I feel proud of myself for getting through and humble at the same time because God has been with me every step of the way.

Nancy Stokkermans

Afterword

I have summed up a lot of experience in the span of a few thousand words. It seems strange to me to have my own life contained between the covers of a book! I have framed a lifetime of experience—good, bad, ugly, and sublime—in the hope that by telling my own stories I can offer some guidance, comfort, or hope to other people.

All of us suffer, and while one person's suffering is different from another's, we can learn from one another and share our lessons and wisdom. We can help each other heal. We can grasp each other's hands when our paths intersect. I am honored to have shared my life stories with you, and I humbly hope you can learn from both my failures and my successes.

My story doesn't end with the period at the end of this chapter, however. It goes on, well past the bibliography and the dust jacket. It leaps right off the bookshelf and wends along the path I continue to follow. In fact, my own path has recently taken me to Brazil, where I immersed myself in the teachings of an inspirational man named Joao Teixeira de Faria, better known to the world as John of God.

John of God is considered to be the most powerful healer alive today. He has been healing for more than forty years with incredible results. He makes it very clear that it is God who is the true healer; John of God is merely the vessel. After reading about the work of John of God, I decided to go to Brazil and experience for myself the incredible connection this man has with God.

In my next book, I will chronicle my experiences in Brazil and will delve into the lessons I learned while studying the work of John of God. I feel that his messages are deeply aligned with my own and that my own life story is entwined with the story of his healing.

In fact, in the weeks leading up to and following my experiences with John of God, I discovered a new level of healing in my own life. As I prepared for Brazil, I was anxious and excited. I wasn't sure what to do with myself, and so I prayed regularly, asking God to help me clear my mind. I focused. I moved the clutter out of my psyche; I turned down the mental noise. When I got to a place where I could truly concentrate, I found that what my mind really wanted to do was write. To write and write and write.

What flowed from my pen were words about my mother. They were words about my mother on Sunday afternoons. I hadn't known that these words were in there. I hadn't known that they needed to come out. This was a time of intense healing, and this was how I was doing it. I wrote about my mother on Sunday mornings, crying, sobbing into a dirty dishrag, her hair stringy and dank. I wrote about standing behind her as she sat in a plain wood chair in an empty room. I wrote about how she would stare out the window at the bare field beyond our house, about how I would see her shoulders shake with sobs, about how I would be too scared to approach her. I wrote about watching the sun set on a Sunday evening and hearing my mother in the next room, desolately doing the dishes. I wrote about seeing her through the crack of her bedroom door as she climbed into bed next to the snoring body of my father, a man who could never give her anything. I wrote about the love and pity I felt then. These were feelings I had forgotten. I wrote about my mother, and I felt myself heal. I wonder if she will ever heal. I recently had the opportunity to have a loving talk with my mother in her nursing home. We chatted about the past and how she felt during this entire trauma. I was extremely enlightened when she did not pretend that abuse did not happen in my past; I asked my mother why she hurt Kathy so much? She sat in her chair and just looked into space and finally answered "Kathy would not listen. She was stubborn and would not listen. She was disobedient, and your father would not help me at all to discipline her. He would not help me at all. He never changed one diaper when you were a baby, and it was so busy." At that moment I felt tremendous sadness for her, I knew she had felt alone and frustrated even though she had a house full of children. I believe that God is helping my mother heal and she is sorry for what she had done. I forgive you, Mom, for all of the pain you inflicted on us, and I am acutely sorry for all the pain that you endured.

I also find this healing taking place within my mother as I write the last words of this book. A coincidence? I do not think so. This conversation with my mother had come up several times during the drafts of my manuscript without any progress. Now, as the words come to an end, my mother seems healed. I know that God is the healer in this miracle.

I have survived all the Sundays in my life. I have survived the Sundays of my childhood when my family's domestic anguish was at its worst. I have survived the Sundays of my adulthood, when the wan routine of the church Sabbath felt empty and futile. I also learned that my God did cry with me when my mother hit me. He cries with me, but He also laughs along with my silliness. I have moved past these difficult days, have told my story, and have woken up to a new morning. Now, the sun rises on my path, illuminating the details around me. I follow this path toward God, the light, and tomorrow.

Destiny is no matter of chance.
It is a matter of choice.
It is not a thing to be waited for, it is a thing to be achieved.

William Jennings Bryan

Turnbull children
from left to right: Karen, Donna, Ken, Nancy, Kathy & Gordon

Turnbull children and pets having fun outside

Lord, Did You Cry With Me When Mommy Hit Me?

Mother and me
(note the large lump on my forehead and the black eyes)

Kathy and Cindy eating a candy apple after the local fair

Kathy sitting on the back porch alone

Dad

Cindy combing my dad's hair

Cindy Lou all grown up

Selected Books from MSI Press

365 Teacher Secrets for Student Success in Elementary School: A Guide to Ideas and Activities for Parents

A Believer-in-Waiting's First Encounters with God

Blest Atheist

El Poder de lo Transpersonal

Forget the Goal, the Journey Counts…71 Jobs Later

Healing from Incest: Frank Conversations of a Victim with Her Therapist

Joshuanism

Las Historias de Mi Vida

Losing My Voice and Finding Another

Mommy Posioned Our House Guest

Publishing for Smarties: How to Find a Publisher

Puertas a la Eternidad

Road to Damascus

The Gospel of Damascus

The Marriage Whisperer

The Rise & Fall of Muslim Civil Society

The Rose and the Sword: Balancing Your Feminine and Masculine Energies

The Seven Wisdoms of Life

Syrian Folktales

Understanding the People Around You: An Introduction to Socionics

When You're Shoved from the Right, Look to the Left: Metaphors of Islamic Humanism

Widow A Survival Guide for the First Year

CPSIA information can be obtained at www.ICGtesting.com
Printed in the USA
LVOW07s0552190913

353059LV00005B/12/P